Praise for
Shattered Dreams

"Making my own plans, setting my own goals, promoting my own agenda, nurturing my own ambition—in short living out my own dreams—are sure ways to get less than God wants to give me. Therefore, I praise God for shattering my dreams…and I praise God for Larry Crabb, who has courageously, clearly, and compassionately defined a biblical principle that is largely misunderstood."

—ANNE GRAHAM LOTZ
author of *Just Give Me Jesus*

"For those of you who want to be as real as God intended you to be, you will want to hold on to every word that Larry Crabb has written in his new book, *Shattered Dreams*. It ministered to my heart—my longing to know God rather than use Him. *Shattered Dreams* is intended to take genuine seekers of truth through a discovery of true hope that will generate a 'new unfamiliar feeling that we will eventually recognize as joy.'"

—DR. CHARLES STANLEY
senior pastor, First Baptist Church Atlanta

"It has been a delight to watch Larry Crabb continue his journey down the path toward a mature and honest spirituality. I look on him as an advance scout in places I have yet to venture."

—PHILIP YANCEY
author of *Reaching for the Invisible God* and
What's So Amazing About Grace?

D1471901

"I've lost count of how many times God has used Larry Crabb to tinker with my interior world. Five pages into this book I muttered to myself, 'Here we go again.'"

—BILL HYBELS

senior pastor of Willow Creek Community Church

"Anyone who knows Larry Crabb knows he's on an extraordinary journey, deep into the soul. And through his recent books—especially this one—we readers are privileged to tag along as Larry brings us to yet another level. He shows us a place where we are sure to encounter the core of our being. And it's here that he teaches us to connect with each other and with God more meaningfully than we ever imagined possible. Through *Shattered Dreams,* Larry skillfully guides us on a transforming journey toward joy—a journey you surely do not want to miss."

—LES PARROTT, PH.D.

author of *When Bad Things Happen to Good Marriages*

"I am pleased to recommend Larry Crabb's work. His commitment to bringing practical guidance and personal passion to the table, enabling others to find and grow in God's best purposes for their lives, makes me thankful for his writings and work."

—JACK W. HAYFORD

founding pastor of The Church on the Way and

chancellor of The King's College and Seminary

"We all know that every cloud has a silver lining, but finding and experiencing it is often an elusive pursuit. Thankfully, Larry Crabb teaches us how to locate and embrace the 'silver' biblically, practically, and penetratingly. For all of us who have been blessed by Larry's ministry, this may be his best work yet."

—DR. JOSEPH M. STOWELL

president of Moody Bible Institute

COMMUNITY
COUNSELLING
SCHOOL

SHATTERED
DREAMS
WORKBOOK

GOD'S

UNEXPECTED

PATHWAY TO JOY

LARRY CRABB

WATERBROOK
PRESS

SHATTERED DREAMS WORKBOOK
PUBLISHED BY WATERBROOK PRESS
2375 Telstar Drive, Suite 160
Colorado Springs, Colorado 80920
A division of Random House, Inc.

Quotations from *Shattered Dreams:* © 2001 by Lawrence J. Crabb Jr., Ph.D., P.C.

All Scripture quotations, unless otherwise indicated, are taken from the *Holy Bible, New International Version®*. NIV®. Copyright © 1973, 1978, 1984 by International Bible Society. Used by permission of Zondervan Publishing House. All rights reserved. Scripture quotations marked (MSG) are taken from *The Message*. Copyright © by Eugene H. Peterson 1993, 1994, 1995. Used by permission of NavPress Publishing Group.

Italics in Scripture quotations reflect the author's added emphasis.

ISBN 1-57856-505-7

Published in association with Yates & Yates, LLP, Literary Agent, Orange, California.

Library of Congress Cataloging-in-Publication Data
Crabb, Lawrence J.
    Shattered dreams workbook / by Larry Crabb.—1st ed.
        p. cm.
    ISBN 1-57856-505-7
    1. Spiritual life—Christianity. 2. Christian life. I. Crabb, Lawrence J. Shattered dreams.
II. Title.

BV4501.3 .C73 2001
248.8'6—dc21

2001026278

Printed in the United States of America
2001

10 9 8 7 6 5 4 3 2

CONTENTS

QUESTIONS YOU MAY HAVE
ABOUT THIS WORKBOOK

What will the *Shattered Dreams Workbook* do for me?

The message from Dr. Larry Crabb in this *Shattered Dreams Workbook* is about discovering God when life isn't "working." It's also about discovering sacred opportunities to experience joy.

This workbook will help you—in a practical and carefully reflective way—to look *through* life's disappointments and tragedies and to see, as never before, just how lavishly God is blessing you, for *His* pleasure as well as for your own.

It will help you understand and release your truest and deepest desires in life and to realize God's surprising ways of putting you in touch with these desires. You'll see how God moves His children from shattered dreams to better dreams—to the highest dream and the joy that comes from dreaming it.

Is this workbook enough, or do I also need the book *Shattered Dreams?*

Although your best approach is to read the book *Shattered Dreams* as you go through this companion workbook, many key portions from the text of *Shattered Dreams* are included here to give you a sufficiently broad and accurate indication of the book's content.

If you do decide to read *Shattered Dreams* as you go through this workbook, you'll find the appropriate chapters to read listed at the beginning of each weekly lesson.

The lessons look long. Do I need to work through all of each one?

This eight-lesson workbook is designed to promote your thorough exploration of each week's material, but you may find it best to focus your time and discussion on some sections and questions more than others.

Also, you may decide to follow a slower pace than one lesson per week. This could be true whether you're going through the workbook individually or in a group. In a group that meets weekly, for example, you may decide to spend two weeks of discussion time on each lesson. (In your first meeting, decide together on what you believe to be the best pacing and schedule.) If you're going through the workbook on your own, you may simply want to try completing two or three questions each day.

Above all, keep in mind that the purpose of the workbook is to help guide you in specific life-application of the biblical truths taught in *Shattered Dreams*. The wide assortment of questions included in each weekly lesson is meant to help you approach this practical application from different angles and with expansive reflection and self-examination.

Allowing adequate time to prayerfully reflect on each question will be much more valuable for you than rushing through this workbook.

However your life is going—
whether you're in a season of blessing or a season of pain—
I invite you to join me on this journey to joy,
to live beyond shattered dreams.
The road will take us through some dark nights,
but you need not wait for morning to rejoice. Morning will come,
but you can welcome your suffering now as an opportunity to meet God,
to encounter Him with a passion that will free you
to get close to a few people in authentic community
and to experience genuine transformation in your personal life,
especially in the way you love others.

—from the introduction in *Shattered Dreams* by Dr. Larry Crabb

OUR PROBLEM
WITH GOD

THIS WEEK'S LESSON IS BASED ON

THE INTRODUCTORY MATERIAL

("A NEW WAY" AND "THE PARABLE")

PLUS CHAPTER 1, "MY PROBLEM WITH GOD,"

IN **SHATTERED DREAMS** BY DR. LARRY CRABB.

As you begin, ask for the Holy Spirit's help in hearing and obeying His words for you at this time.

(Included in each weekly study you'll find a number of excerpts from the book *Shattered Dreams,* each one marked at the beginning and end by this symbol: 📖. These excerpts serve not only to convey Dr. Crabb's message from the book, but also to stimulate your reflection and discussion and to guide your exploration of Scripture. The excerpts are usually brief, so you may want to frequently refer back to the book *Shattered Dreams* and review their fuller context.)

God's Longing and Ours

In his introduction, Dr. Crabb tells of three ideas that filled his mind as he wrote the book *Shattered Dreams.* Think about these ideas as presented in the following quotations, then respond to the questions below each one.

1. The first idea:

> 📖 *God wants to bless you.* He gets a kick out of making His children happy. He feels much the same way parents feel on Christmas morning as they anticipate watching their kids unwrap presents amid squeals of delight....
>
> There's never a moment in all our lives, from the day we trusted Christ till the day we see Him, when God is not longing to bless us. At every moment, in every circumstance, God is doing us good. He never stops. It gives Him too much pleasure. God is not waiting to bless us after our troubles end. He is blessing us right now, in and through those troubles. At this exact moment, He is giving us what He thinks is good. 📖

What is your response to the basic idea expressed in the preceding quotation? How fully do you accept and believe it? What doubts or questions, if any, does it raise in your mind?

2. The second idea:

> 📖 *The deepest pleasure we're capable of experiencing is a direct encounter with God.* In God's new way of dealing with people, He does us the most good by making Himself available to be enjoyed and by seeing to it that we seek an encounter with Him with more energy than we seek anything else....

The highest dream we could ever dream, the wish that if granted would make us happier than any other blessing, is to know God, to actually experience Him. 📖

How do you respond to this idea? How fully do you accept and believe it? Does it raise any doubts or questions in your mind?

3. The third idea:

📖 The problem is that we don't believe this idea [that encountering God is our deepest pleasure].... We assent to it in our heads. But we don't feel it in our hearts....

So the Holy Spirit awakens that appetite. *He uses the pain of shattered dreams to help us discover our desire for God,* to help us begin dreaming the highest dream....

Our shattered dreams are never random. They are always a piece in a larger puzzle, a chapter in a larger story. 📖

Once more, what is your response to this idea? How fully do you accept and believe it? What doubts or questions does it raise in your mind?

4. Following the introduction in *Shattered Dreams* is a section entitled "The Parable." It's reprinted, in full, beginning on page 144 near the end of this workbook. Read this short section now.

How would you summarize what happens to the man in "The Parable"?

In your own words, how would you express the message or point of this parable?

Your Best Friend?

5. Dr. Crabb tells about jotting down a list of his best friends.

📖 I'm looking at the names I wrote. One impression strikes me at once with near gale force. *The friends who made the list are all friends who do something for me.* It's not what I do for them that got them on the list; it's what they do for me....

The people on my list respond to my concerns. They use their resources on my behalf. When I have a need, they meet it if they can. I like that about them....

So I'm left with an obvious fact. The people I most cherish in all the world are the people I can count on to do for me what I most want. I suspect if you wrote down the names of the six people whose friendship you most value, that same fact might be obvious to you. 📖

After questioning whether this fact proves that we're all "hopelessly mired in disgusting self-centeredness," Dr. Crabb then realizes that it never occurred to him to put God's name on his best-friends list.

📖 Sometimes God seems like the least responsive friend I have.… Depending on an unresponsive God in the middle of crumbling dreams can be tough on faith. Relating personally with a God who is less responsive than friends with far fewer resources is difficult. 📖

In what ways, if any, have your impressions and concerns been similar to what is expressed above?

Like a Little Child

6. Dr. Crabb's words in the following quotation reflect his thoughts on Luke 18:17, where Jesus speaks of receiving the kingdom of God "like a little child."

📖 [Jesus] wants us to humble ourselves, to let someone know when we could really use a hug or some quality time, to let the Spirit know we need Him to change our hearts, to confess to our community of close friends the weaknesses we should have resolved by now.

I hear Jesus telling us to stop negotiating with Him, to stop offering something we think we have in exchange for His blessings.… "All you can do is receive what you need from someone who has what you don't. When you admit your emptiness, I'll see to it you're filled." 📖

In keeping with this childlike openness and dependence, how would you express some of your own personal needs or emptiness that you can honestly bring to Jesus today?

7. Keep these perspectives on childlikeness in mind as you choose to explore any of the following familiar passages. Reflect on them in a fresh way, then feel free to express in your own words (a) the message they give us and (b) your response to that message.

Psalm 145:18-19

Matthew 11:28

Hebrews 4:16

Hebrews 10:22

James 4:8-10

8. Dr. Crabb points to our self-protective tendencies as he mentions "the first commandment of fallen thinking," stated in these words: "Trust no one and you shall live." In what ways, if any, have you adopted and followed such a "commandment" in your life?

9. Now consider the "second commandment of fallen thinking," which Dr. Crabb expresses in these words: "To make life work, trust only yourself and what you can control." To what extent have you ever followed this approach to life?

Taste and See

📖 We evangelicals speak about having a personal relationship with Jesus. We hold out the possibility of having a really good relationship with Him. If that relationship hits a snag or develops tension, we know it's always our doing. Since I was a child, I've heard the saying, "If you're not feeling close to God, guess who moved?" The message was clear: Every difficulty in our relationship with God is always our fault. It's never His.

But especially in the years since I turned fifty, that message has not always seemed so obvious. 📖

10. What has been your own belief regarding the issue addressed in the preceding quotation? If there's tension or distance in your relationship with God, have you viewed this as being always your own "fault"? Why or why not?

\

📖 When we see things rightly, we'll write His name in capital letters at the top of our list of friends and, with the angels, bow low before Him in adoration and awe. And hope. I believe that.

But it takes some doing to see things rightly. 📖

11. What do you think we may need most in order to "see things rightly," so that God's name is at the top of our list of friends?

12. In the early pages of *Shattered Dreams,* Dr. Crabb writes this:

📖 This book is an invitation to taste and see that the Lord is good even when the bottom falls out of your life....

How can we write His name at the top of our list as the most wonderful, most sensitive, and most responsive friend we've ever had when our fondest dreams shatter and He does nothing? That's the question I'll try to answer in this book. 📖

With those words in mind, how would you express your personal goals or expectations for the time you'll spend going through the *Shattered Dreams Workbook*?

13. In quietness, review what you have written and learned in this week's lesson. If further thoughts or prayer requests come to your mind and heart, you may want to write them here.

14. What for you was the most meaningful concept or truth in this week's lesson?

    How would you talk this over with God? Write your response here as a prayer to Him.

    What do you believe God wants you to do in response to this week's study?

TRUSTING GOD IS DANGEROUS BUSINESS

THIS WEEK'S LESSON IS BASED ON

CHAPTER 2, "WE NEED A GOOD STORY,"

CHAPTER 3, "JESUS SPEAKS,"

AND CHAPTER 4, "WHEN BOTH SHOES DROP,"

IN **SHATTERED DREAMS** BY DR. LARRY CRABB.

In this lesson we begin seeking what Dr. Crabb calls "a hope that has the power to do something truly wonderful when the dark night descends and we see nothing but pain and disappointment in this life, a hope that does exactly the same thing when the sky is sunny."

As you begin, remember to ask for the Holy Spirit's help in hearing and obeying His words for you at this time.

Handle the Pain

Dr. Crabb reminds us in his book that we all go through the experience of shattered dreams in one form or another—"if not yesterday then today, if not today then tomorrow. How do we respond? What happens in us when life throws an unexpected curve our way, when the second shoe drops soon after the first?"

This is the central question we want to ask ourselves in this week's study.

1. For many of us, the response is captured in these words:

> 📖 *Handle pain!* Find some way to keep going in spite of the hurt. Don't think about it. Stay strong, move on to the next chapter, make it. Do whatever helps, whether going on a spiritual retreat, leaning on family, talking to a counselor, or reading books recommended by concerned friends. Relieve the pain if you can. Live through it if you must. Whatever you do, handle the pain! 📖

In what ways has this ever been your own response to shattered dreams? And how would you evaluate that response, as best you can, from God's perspective?

> 📖 In our struggle to handle the pain of shattered dreams, however, one question is rarely talked about with honesty.... The question is this: *What do we do with how we're feeling toward God?* What we want is good; it's not selfish. Why won't God let us have it?...
>
> Why is God so inconsistent, so maddeningly unpredictable?... Why? Suffering seems so random; one dream realized, another shattered. 📖

2. Think back to times when you've squarely faced the shattering of your dreams. In those moments, what were your feelings toward God?

3. Look up some of the verses listed below from the Psalms (or similar passages you know). In what ways and to what extent do these inspired words of Scripture mirror feelings that you have experienced?

10:1

13:1-2

22:1

43:2

69:2-3

88:14

A Story of Shattered Dreams

In chapter 2 of *Shattered Dreams,* Dr. Crabb writes this:

> 📖 After I properly set the stage, I want to tell a story. Actually, I want to retell an old familiar story, one already told in the Old Testament book of Ruth. Recently, through my own experience with shattered dreams, I've come to the conclusion that the story of Naomi was written to answer the question I'm asking.... *How do we trust a sometimes disappointing, seemingly fickle God who fails to do for us what good friends, if they could, would do?* 📖

Naomi's story, says Dr. Crabb, "solves my problem with God." We'll be exploring that story as presented in the brief book of Ruth (all four chapters are reprinted in the back of this workbook).

4. Begin your fresh encounter with Naomi's story by reading through the first chapter of Ruth. As a helpful exercise for deepening your grasp of the story, write here a concise outline of the events in Naomi's life as told in Ruth 1.

5. In this first chapter of the book of Ruth, how do you see Naomi responding to shattered dreams?

6. Below are comments from Dr. Crabb about the way Naomi's story begins in Ruth 1. Below each comment, record how it relates to your own observations of this passage. List also any relevant questions that come to your mind.

📖 The Lord could have done something. And He did nothing. How else could she think?

Her husband and both sons, all three dead. And yet God is the God of the impossible. He can do anything.

But He did nothing.

Sometimes He does come through. Naomi knew the stories. I wonder if her mind roamed back through her nation's history, maybe to the story of Abraham, a favorite among her people. 📖

📖 Naomi, with a good husband and two fine sons, was full of hope when together they left Bethlehem. The famine there had prompted a move to Moab. Naomi assumed—it was less a dream and more an assumption—that a short stay in Moab would go well, and then, when the rains came, she would return to Bethlehem *with* her husband, *with* her two sons, perhaps *with* a couple of daughters-in-law.

After all, in a recent battle with Israel, Moab had lost thousands of eligible young men. Pickings for her boys might be good. Had she thought about it, Naomi would have naturally reasoned that bringing her family back home, happy and intact, was easy compared to arranging for a ninety-year-old woman to conceive. But God's surprises aren't always pleasant. Naomi learned that lesson with force. 📖

📖 Naomi's husband, Elimelech, passed away shortly after they reached Moab. One dream shattered. But then her two sons met nice girls and married. Perhaps she thought, as we all do, that if the other shoe did not drop, she would be able to get on. If enough blessings come along to enjoy, perhaps we can endure the pain. God knows we couldn't handle one more trial. And He gave His word we would never be asked to suffer more than we could endure. Then *that* becomes our dream—that sufficient blessings would come our way to get us through.

Then the other shoe dropped. Both her sons died. We're not told how. The Lord could have kept them alive; that much we know. But He didn't. 📖

When the Fire Goes Out

📖 When dreams shatter, we lose hope. We may get on, but the fire is out. There may still be some things worth living for, but the best is gone. The spark has been doused, our passion for life extinguished. At least that's how it seems....

How do we find the faith that lets us see what is invisible, to passionately believe that He's always wonderfully and lovingly responsive when He seems so callous? That's the question: *What does it mean to hope in God as we continue to live in a world where good dreams shatter and God seems to do nothing about it?* 📖

7. At this season in your life, how would you answer the final question posed in the preceding quotation?

📖 Trusting God is dangerous business. Unless we're trusting Him for what He's promised to provide, the step after trust is disillusionment....

So what *can* He be trusted for? Exactly what is He doing with His considerable power? What would be different if we experienced that power, if His power were released in us? 📖

8. Again, how would you answer the questions in the preceding quotation, to the best of your understanding today?

📖 There is an answer, and it is repeated again and again in the Bible. But the answer, the only one that squarely faces the enormous challenge of trusting a seemingly unresponsive God, requires a change in how we naturally look at life. It demands a revolution in our understanding of why we're alive at all, of why God keeps us living in this world for so long before He takes us to heaven. 📖

9. How would you evaluate your present ability to take on a "revolution" in your thinking about God, as called for above? How open are you to thinking in ways drastically different from your accustomed thought patterns? On what basis and by what criteria can you gauge this openness within yourself?

📖 Is the only point to godly living the reward we'll receive in heaven? Is there anything we can hope for now, anything we can count on God to do for us in this life? That's the question. And it's not a selfish one, it's a humble one, a question that admits we're dependent children in need of receiving what we long for but do not have. Our souls need filling. 📖

10. The second sentence in the above quotation pinpoints another crucial question in our relationship with God. How would you answer it, according to your current understanding of Scripture?

A Different Kind of Hope

11. From Hebrews 11, Dr. Crabb draws the following conclusion: "Apparently God is pleased with people who suffer terribly, whose lives never straighten out, but who keep trusting." As you look over Hebrews 11 for yourself, what portions of it lead you to the same conclusion? What other significant conclusions can you draw from this passage that may pertain to this week's topic?

12. In the following quotation, we find a much different approach to life than the one taught in Hebrews 11.

> 📖 More than perhaps ever before in history, we assume we are here for one fundamental reason: *to have a good time*—if not good circumstances, then at least good feelings. We long to feel alive, to sense passion and romance and freedom. We want the good time of enjoying godly kids, of making a difference in people's lives, of involvement with close friends, of experiencing God's peace. So we invent "biblical" strategies for seeing to it that our dreams come true. We call them models of godly parenting and disciplines of spiritual living and principles of financial stewardship—all designed to give us a legitimately good time. What's wrong with that?
>
> But when we uncover the deepest motives that drive our actions, we discover a determination to feel *now* what no one will feel until heaven. 📖

In what ways—and how strongly—can you identify with the feelings and motives described in the words above?

> 📖 What God has in mind when He tells us to keep hoping may not be what we usually mean when we think of hope. We wish for things to get better; we want to feel what we want to feel.

Those are our dreams. But that kind of hope is for later. For now, in this life, the Bible offers a different kind of hope, a kind that at first we don't find attractive or even hopeful....

The best hope, our highest dream of being in His presence where nothing ever goes wrong and where we fully enjoy Him more than every other blessing, will not be granted till the next life. 📖

13. To what degree, if any, might you be seeking fulfillment in this life for hopes that won't be granted until eternity? What are these hopes?

14. When our life's purpose "is to have a good time, to have soul-pleasure exceed soul-pain," Dr. Crabb writes, "God becomes merely a means to an end, an object to be used, never a subject rightfully demanding a response, never a lover to be enjoyed." To what extent might this have been true in your life in the past, or even in the present?

📖 It's harder to discover our desire for God when things go well. We may think we have, but more often all we've found is our desire to *use* God, not to *enjoy* Him. Shattered dreams are the truest blessings; they help us discover our true hope. But it can take a long, dark time to discover it.... Shattered dreams open the door to better

dreams, dreams that we do not properly value until the dreams that
we improperly value are destroyed. Shattered dreams destroy false
expectations, such as the "victorious" Christian life with no real
struggle or failure. They help us discover true hope. We need the
help of shattered dreams to put us in touch with what we most long
for, to create a felt appetite for better dreams. And living for the better dreams generates a new, unfamiliar feeling that we eventually
recognize as joy. 📖

15. How fully do you agree with the statements about shattered dreams in the
preceding quotation? To what extent have you come to any of these same
conclusions on your own?

Jesus Speaks

16. Dr. Crabb portrays the Mount of Olives as a "Place of Hope" for Jesus,
despite the agony of His prayers there on the night before He was crucified.
Explore Luke 22:39-53 and Acts 1:6-12 (you may also want to refer also to
Zechariah 14:3-5 and Matthew 24) to find the verses that speak most directly
to what Jesus wanted His followers to learn from their experience with Him
in this place.

How would you summarize those lessons? And how do they relate to the topic of this week's study?

17. In a chapter of *Shattered Dreams* entitled "Jesus Speaks," Dr. Crabb writes: "Drawing from all that we have now considered, I hear Him speaking words like these to us. Listen."

    These words are listed below. Read them reflectively, accepting each paragraph, as you're able, as the Lord's personal communication to you. Then choose one or more of the paragraphs and record your prayerful response.

    📖 Some of your fondest dreams will shatter, and you will be tempted to lose hope. I will seem to you callous or, worse, weak—unresponsive to your pain. You will wonder if I cannot do anything or simply will not. 📖

    📖 As you struggle with dashed hopes, you will fail, just as My servant Peter did. You will feel discouraged with yourself to the point of self-hatred. And I will seem to withdraw from you and do nothing. 📖

📖 When all of this comes to pass, My word to you is this: *Do not lose hope.* A plan is unfolding that you cannot clearly see. If you could see it as I do, you would still hurt, but you would not lose hope. You would gladly remain faithful to me in the middle of the worst suffering. I guarantee you the power to please me, not to have a good time. But pleasing me will bring you great joy. 📖

📖 In the deepest part of your soul, you long more than anything else to be a part of My plan, to further My kingdom, to know Me and please Me and enjoy Me. I will satisfy that longing. You have the power to represent Me well no matter what happens in your life. That is the hope I give you in this world. Don't lose it. 📖

18. In quietness, review what you've written and learned in this week's lesson. If further thoughts or prayer requests come to mind, you may want to write them here.

19. What for you was the most meaningful concept or truth in this week's lesson?

How would you talk this over with God? Write your response here as a prayer to Him.

What do you believe God wants you to do in response to this week's study?

THE PATH OF HOPE

THIS WEEK'S LESSON IS BASED ON

CHAPTER 5, "THE RHYTHM OF HOPE,"

CHAPTER 6, "BREAKING THE RULES,"

AND CHAPTER 7, "HIDDEN HOPE,"

IN SHATTERED DREAMS BY DR. LARRY CRABB.

Hope has its own rhythm," writes Dr. Crabb. "We cannot rush it. The water of life will find its way down the mountain to fill the lake from which we can drink." In this lesson we'll explore this rhythm as well as some other surprising aspects of true hope.

As you begin, remember again to ask for the Holy Spirit's help in hearing and obeying His words for you at this time.

God's Goodness and Our Happiness

Think about your personal definitions for "happiness" and "joy" as you read carefully through the following extended excerpt from *Shattered Dreams*.

> 📖 If given the choice, we would prefer to keep whatever happiness
> we've already found. Like the child who never wants to grow
> beyond the wide-eyed excitement of Christmas morning, we like to
> remain naively happy. Keep the blessings coming. Keep the good

times rolling. When we signed on to the Christian life, that's what we thought was the deal. We do what we're told, and God stacks presents under the tree.

Our experience of happiness is not entirely wrong; it is, however, naive. It is both innocent and shallow, rooted in a strange blend of a child's optimism and a fool's arrogant spirit of entitlement. Things will go well for us; they're supposed to. *Other* people get cancer and suffer through divorce and lose their jobs and experience a friend's betrayal.

With adolescent maturity we declare that God is good when we ace the physics test or finish law school with honors, when our son is offered an unusually good position or the biopsy comes back negative. "Of course," we say, "God is good!" Without putting it quite this way, we assume God is pleased and grateful that we think so— and maybe just a little relieved.

When blessings come, we should of course enjoy them. It's good when children squeal with delight on Christmas morning; it's sad when they can't. Celebrate the good things of life. Enjoy the juicy steak, the unexpected bonus, the beautiful granddaughter.

Happy people, though they're right to be happy, face a subtle danger. They tend to spiritually gloat, to publicly express gratitude and praise for the good things they enjoy while privately thinking that blessings are their due. They can easily slip into a concern for the less fortunate that carries with it a mood of judgment: *If they were more like me, they would be given the blessings I have.* We don't easily recognize that mood within ourselves.

Unhappy folks face their own unique temptation. Publicly they tell the more fortunate how glad they are for all who are so blessed; privately they wish that the happy person's path would hit a ditch.

Rejoice with those who rejoice and weep with those who weep. No command is more difficult to obey. Beneath the surface, we lament another's joy (that's the sin of jealousy) and feel good when a much blessed friend has reason to cry (that's the sin of smugness, a close cousin of jealousy).

Happy people do not love well. Joyful people do. That's why happiness, the pleasant feelings that pleasant circumstances generate, must be taken away in order to be replaced by joy.

Happy people rarely look for joy. They're quite content with what they have. The foundation of their life consists of the blessings they enjoy. Although they may genuinely care about those less fortunate and do great things to help, their central concern is to keep what they have. They haven't been freed to pursue a greater dream. That's why they cannot love well. In His severe mercy, God takes away the good to create an appetite for the better, and then, eventually, He satisfies the new appetite, liberating them to love. 📖

1. What statements or descriptions in the above selection can you most identify with, and why?

How would you describe, as fully as possible, your own view of happiness?

How would you describe your understanding of true joy?

2. "It comes down to this," Dr. Crabb says:

📖 God's best is available only to those who sacrifice, or who are willing to sacrifice, the merely good. If we are satisfied with good health, responsible children, enjoyable marriages, close friendships, interesting jobs, and successful ministries, we will never hunger for God's best. We will never worship. I've come to believe that only broken people truly worship. Unbroken people—happy folks who enjoy their blessings more than the Blesser—say thanks to God the way a shopper thanks a clerk. 📖

What thoughts come to mind as you read these conclusions? In what ways is it easy for you to agree with them? In what ways do you find it difficult to agree?

Heavy Blessing

📖 List every blessing you desire. Put them all on the left side of a scale. Now list the blessing that we're told is the very highest, an intimate relationship with God. Put that one, by itself, on the right side of the scale.

Do we believe that what is on the right side immediately and decisively outweighs what is on the left? If we did, we would move more quickly from happiness through the agony of shattered dreams to complete joy.

Only a few in any generation believe that the weight of knowing God is a blessing heavier (and by that I mean more wonderful) than every other. And those who believe it appear to have developed that conviction only through suffering. Happiness must be stripped away, forcibly, before joy can surface, before we will value and pursue dreams whose fulfillment produces true joy. 📖

3. What do you think it takes for someone to be totally convinced that knowing God is truly a greater blessing by far than all other blessings? And how important is it to have this conviction?

4. In what ways and to what extent do you see this conviction reflected in any of the following passages?

Psalm 16:2

Psalm 42:1-2

Psalm 73:25-26

Habakkuk 3:17-18

Matthew 10:37

Philippians 3:8

The Rhythm of Hope

5. Take a few moments to review the first chapter of the book of Ruth.

    Dr. Crabb points out "three characteristics of Naomi's despair" that emerge in Ruth 1, characteristics which are "often part of our own journey to hope."

    His summaries of these characteristics are shown below. For each one, list the verse or verses in Ruth 1 where you see this characteristic in Naomi. Feel free to mention also your own impressions of Naomi's despair and to tell about times when you have had similar thoughts.

    📖 First, she believed people would be better off spending time with someone other than herself.... *You're better off without me.* 📖

    📖 Second, she lost all hope of a return to earlier blessings that brought happiness.... *Happiness is only a memory, never to be experienced again.* 📖

    📖 Third, she believed the tragedies were God's doing.... *Tragedies in our lives are God's doing.* Perhaps they come as discipline for our wrong choices or maybe they come for some other reason, but either way, tragedies are God's doing. He could prevent them. He doesn't. 📖

6. At this time in your life, what gives you the most help in patiently following God's "rhythm of hope," as Dr. Crabb expresses it in the following quotation?

> 📖 God is working when we see nothing but darkness. He is moving with rhythmic purpose through our agony and pain to unimaginable joy.
>
> Knowing that He's moving at all sometimes becomes the central piece of faith we need to keep ourselves moving. The courage to not quit, to not settle for immediate pleasure that brings happiness back for only a moment, often depends on our conviction that God is moving, that we are being taken to an experience of ecstasy along a path of suffering, that there is no other way to get there. 📖

7. With honesty, describe the degree of confidence you now have that God indeed is working and moving in your life and in your circumstances at this time.

The Desire Beneath the Pain

📖 The Western church has become a community of either the victorious or the acceptably broken. Either we speak glowingly of our love for Jesus—usually because the blessings are abundant—or we struggle nobly through hard times, convincing others and sometimes ourselves that we're doing better than we are. With each other we're more proper than real, more appropriate than alive....

Could we actually love God so much that we could feel all the pain of a teenage daughter's pregnancy and still worship? Could we still love our daughter? Or do we believe that loving God would somehow reduce the pain that a child's rebellion creates? 📖

8. How would you answer the questions raised in the second paragraph of the preceding quotation?

📖 When you hurt, hurt. Hurt openly in the presence of God. Hurt openly in the presence of the few who provide you with safe community. Feel your pain. Regard brokenness as an opportunity, as the chance to discover a desire that no brokenness can eliminate but that only brokenness reveals.

Remember what brokenness is. It's the awareness that you long to be someone you're not and cannot be without divine help. Never pretend to God, to yourself, or to your safe community that you feel what you don't or that you are what you're not. With everyone else, including Christians attending a Bible conference, choose to be congenial. Not everyone needs to see your brokenness. 📖

9. How do you respond to the advice given in the preceding quotation? How possible would it be for you to fully follow this advice?

10. Revisit some of the familiar biblical passages listed below that relate to handling your own hurts or the hurts of others. In what ways, if any, do you view them differently as a result of this study? In what ways might they communicate more strongly to you than before? Record your thoughts in the space provided.

Romans 12:12-15

1 Corinthians 12:26

2 Corinthians 1:3-5

Galatians 6:2

Ephesians 4:2

Philippians 1:29

Hebrews 13:3

James 1:2-3

1 Peter 1:6-7

Keeping Desire Alive

📖 My growing conviction is that no one discovers the fullness of
their desire for God without entering the fullness of lesser desires....

We must therefore feel the soul-piercing pain of disappointment,
of the imperfect love we've received and the equally imperfect love
we have given. But when all we experience is pain, loneliness, and
despair, we can know with certainty that we have not yet entered
the depths of our souls. Beneath our troubled emotion is a desire for
God that in rich measure can be satisfied now....

>   Don't let your hearts be troubled. In the middle of shattered
> dreams, discover a desire that Christ pledges Himself to satisfy.
> Don't set out to discover that desire. The desire will surface, like
> bubbling water from a spring that can no longer be held back. 📖

11. What do you think it means to "enter the fullness of lesser desires," as this
term is used in the above quotation?

Is it easy for you to agree with the author on this? Why or why not?

Breaking the Rules

12. Think about how you generally respond to others who are experiencing pain
or loss. Dr. Crabb notes that "two unwritten rules eventually surface in our
response to one who hurts."

📖 First, mourning has a time limit…. Second, we think there's a proper way to mourn. Ugly battles should remain out of sight. Acceptable battles may be shared, but only if we season our account with hope. 📖

Then he notes that "Naomi broke both the time-limit rule and the proper-mourning rule." In your own reading of Ruth 1, where do you see Naomi breaking these "rules"?

13. Below is an excerpt of Dr. Crabb's further comments on Naomi's "rule-breaking." Once more, record your own response to his analysis plus any other reflections or questions you have. (You may also want to look once more at Ruth 1 with these fresh thoughts in mind.)

📖 Her husband had died nearly ten years earlier, her sons more recently but still long enough ago that by now she should have gained perspective. But still she was reeling. Where was her faith? Is God good or not? Is He worthy of trust or does He make mistakes? I can see her community pointing fingers while expressing similar admonitions.

And the way she talked about her shattered dreams was unbecoming to a follower of El Shaddai. "Yes, God is an invincible mountain, a force that cannot be resisted. But that is cause for praise, not complaint." Perhaps that's what the elders in Bethlehem told her. It's certainly what many sufferers hear today from their spiritual leaders. No wonder we run off to counselors.

Don't sanitize the story. Naomi did *not* say, "I'm having a hard time. Most nights I cry myself to sleep. But God knows what He's doing. My family died for good reasons that I cannot see but I claim by faith. I know nothing enters my life without passing through His tender hands. My hope is in the Lord."

That may be what we think she should have said, what we wished she had said, but it's not what she did say. She was miserable, and she saw God as the source of her misfortune. 📖

14. At the end of chapter 1 in the book of Ruth, we read that Naomi returned to Bethlehem "as the barley harvest was beginning."

Dr. Crabb notes that this is the first of four "telling phrases" that point to "God's behind-the-scenes movement in Naomi's life." He highlights this first "telling phrase" in these words:

📖 After more than ten years in Moab, Naomi returned to Bethlehem *"as the barley harvest was beginning"* (1:22). The darkest night precedes the brightest dawn. That is not cliché, it is how God works. 📖

In this phrase, he says, "we can see the sun's tip rise above the horizon. Naomi couldn't see it, but it was there. The harvest is coming." Dr. Crabb then adds, "In each of our lives...the harvest is beginning; the sun is rising." What evidence do you see that this process may be happening in your own life at this time—that the harvest is beginning, and the sun is rising? If you don't see that evidence now, can you tell of some time in the past when you were able to see it?

Different Paths

📖 "Don't let your hearts be troubled," He told His disciples. What did Jesus mean? Is He telling us to pretend we feel what we should feel when our most deeply experienced emotions are quite the opposite? Are we to admit our troubled feelings only to ourselves and God, while telling others that God's presence and promises are real to us when they're not? Is Jesus agreeing with Buddha in prescribing a form of contentment that requires us to cut off the nerve endings of our souls and to report peace when what we feel is a void? Is He teaching that if we trust Him, we'll feel no pain? 📖

15. In the past, what has been your own deepest understanding of the command from Jesus to "let not your heart be troubled"?

16. In *Shattered Dreams,* Dr. Crabb mentions "the 'four noble truths' that make up the core of Buddhist teaching":

📖 Truth 1: *Life is suffering.* There is always, in everyone's life, a gap between desire and reality. The gap is suffering.

Truth 2: *The cause of all suffering is desire.* People suffer because they desire what they do not experience. It is not possible to have everything you desire. Therefore, if you desire, you will suffer.

Truth 3: *The way to end suffering is to end desire.* Want nothing, then nothing can disturb you. A person without dreams will never suffer the pain of seeing them shattered.

Truth 4: *Spend your life learning to eliminate desire.* The "eightfold path," the way of Buddha, shows you how. 📖

In what ways have you adopted one or more of these perspectives?

17. Dr. Crabb then compares those "four noble truths" of Buddhism with the fundamentally different path of following Jesus.

    Showing the contrast, he summarizes the teachings of Christ in the following four statements. For each one, think about how fully you recognize and believe it. Record your responses and reflective thoughts:

    📖 Truth 1: *Life includes suffering, but life is good.* In this world, His followers and everyone else will suffer tribulation. But Jesus has made a way for us to satisfy our deepest desire in the midst of unrelieved pain. 📖

    📖 Truth 2: *The cause of all suffering is separation.* We are separated from God—and from our own deepest desire, our longing for God—and we're therefore deceived into looking elsewhere for joy. That sets us off on the ultimate wild goose chase. Nothing but God satisfies our most profound desire. 📖

📖 Truth 3: *The way to handle suffering is to discover your desire for God.* Then everything, both good and bad, becomes redemptive. It moves us toward the God we desire. Enter your thirst. Feel your ache, the very worst ache that throbs in your soul. Face how you harm others, your spouse, your children, your friends. And face your disappointment with them. Eventually, you will seek God for…

…forgiveness of your failure to love.

…the love you desire.

…empowerment to love others.

…hope that one day you will revel in love freely given and freely received in a perfect community of lovers. 📖

📖 Truth 4: *The new life provided through Jesus must be accepted as a gift of love.* We then spend the rest of our days discovering our desire to know God better, and we come to realize it's a desire whose satisfaction no shattered dream can thwart. 📖

18. In quietness, review what you've written and learned in this week's lesson. If further thoughts or prayer requests come to mind, you may want to record them here.

19. What for you was the most meaningful concept or truth in this week's lesson?

   How would you talk this over with God? Write your response here as a prayer to Him.

   What do you believe God wants you to do in response to this week's study?

GOD IS MOVING

THIS WEEK'S LESSON IS BASED ON
CHAPTER 8, "EVERYTHING HELPS ME TO GOD,"
CHAPTER 9, "DESIRE OR ADDICTION?"
AND CHAPTER 10, "THE ELUSIVE GOD,"
IN **SHATTERED DREAMS** BY DR. LARRY CRABB.

A s you begin, remember again to ask for the Holy Spirit's help in hearing and obeying His words for you at this time.

📖 If you're seeking God in the middle of shattered dreams, if you've become aware of your desire for Him but are having trouble finding Him, be encouraged that it bothers you. The more you're bothered by not finding Him, the more aware you're becoming of how badly you want Him. Abandon yourself to Him. Let the Cross bring you confidence that He is with you and will reveal Himself to you. Abandonment and confidence—here are two key elements of true spirituality. 📖

Everything Helps Me to God

1. Chapter 8 in *Shattered Dreams* is entitled "Everything Helps Me to God," a quote from the French spiritual guide Jean-Pierre de Caussade.

📖 It's his way of saying what Paul taught two thousand years ago, that all things—a spouse's death, a son's rebellion, a missed career—*all things,* in the hand of God, work together for good for people whose primary agenda is to glorify God, who long to enjoy Him as they enjoy no one else and to reveal Him to others in every relational encounter....

Do you believe that everything helps a person to God, including a suicidal son, a devastating divorce, a secret moral failure, an unfulfilling job? If so, how do you preach what you believe? 📖

How would you answer the questions in the last paragraph of the quotation above?

Counseling Naomi

2. Dr. Crabb summarizes Naomi's situation at the end of Ruth 1 in these words:

📖 She's not doing well. Life has been hard. Ten years ago she was widowed; a few years later she lost both her married sons before either had fathered a child; now she has returned home with a nice young woman, a daughter-in-law from the despised country of Moab. Naomi is no longer young, her money is gone, her property is sold, she can't manage to shake off feelings of depression, and she is mad at God, convinced that she has been a victim of His ruthless sovereignty. 📖

He then asks you to assume that Naomi attends a church of which you are the pastor.

📖 What will you say in next Sunday's sermon that you honestly believe she might hear? What message could you preach that the Spirit might use to draw her along on the path toward God?… Or assume you're a Christian counselor. Ruth has brought Naomi to your office, then waits outside to let you do whatever you do with depressed clients. What would you say to this slumped-over old lady? 📖

Think back to where you were in your spiritual understanding and experience two or three years ago. If you were Naomi's pastor or counselor at that time, what would you most likely have said to her?

What might you say differently to Naomi *today*, as her pastor or counselor?

📖 Our generation has lost the concept of finding joy in unfulfilled desire. We no longer know what it means to hope. We want what we want *now*....

Impatient Westerners prefer quick sanctification. Take your car into the shop and drive it again the next day. Bring your soul to a counselor or pastor and get fixed right away.

But wisdom understands that souls are not broken machines that experts fix. Wisdom knows the deep workings of the hungry, hurting, sin-inclined soul and patiently follows as the Spirit moves quietly in those depths, gently nudging people toward God.

There is no Concorde that flies us from immaturity to maturity in a few hours. There is only a narrow, bumpy road where a few people walk together as they journey to God. 📖

3. In your own life, how much do you think impatience and an inability to hope might be factors in slowing your progress in knowing God?

4. If impatience and a shortage of hope are indeed obstacles in your spiritual life, how can they be removed? Consider the possibility that they cannot be removed but only overcome. If that's true, *how* can they be overcome?

The Gift of Inadequacy

For years I hid the inadequacy I felt as a counselor behind a professional demeanor, technical jargon, and sound psychological methods of treatment. Recently I've made a truly liberating discovery. I *am* inadequate. My sense of inadequacy is not the effect of deficient intellect or poor training, nor is it a symptom of emotional disorder. It is the painful admission of what is true. On my own, I can make nothing of importance happen. I can help no one.

But if I abide in Christ, if I present myself before God's Spirit for searching and filling, if I study and ponder the Scriptures and live my life in brokenness before a grace-dispensing community, I can transcend my inadequacy. I can find myself as I worship. I can struggle on behalf of others with the energy of Christ powerfully working in me.

I have learned that an awareness of inadequacy is neither a curse to lift nor a disorder to cure. It is a gift to be received, a gift that if properly used can make me powerful and strong and clear and wise.

5. In what significant ways have you recognized your own inadequacy, particularly in relating effectively in another person's life?

6. In practical, everyday terms, what do you think it might mean to properly accept and use your inadequacy as a gift? Think about this question especially in the context of significant relationships, not tasks.

Naomi's Story Continues

📖 God was at work when He brought Naomi home "as the barley harvest was beginning." But His work was not visible. The night was still dark. Naomi was discouraged and depressed. But if we listen carefully as her story unfolds, we can hear God whispering that dawn is on its way. The harvest is beginning. A better dream is about to be revealed—and fulfilled. 📖

7. Read carefully the second chapter of Ruth, and write a concise outline of the events narrated there.

8. In the second chapter of Ruth, Dr. Crabb finds another "telling phrase" to indicate God's behind-the-scenes movement in Naomi's journey to joy:

> 📖 Ruth asked her depressed, inactive mother-in-law for permission to "go to the fields and pick up the leftover grain"; and so, "*as it turned out,* she found herself working in a field belonging to Boaz" (2:2-3). Deliverance from despair always comes through a person. It was no mere stroke of good luck that, "as it turned out," Ruth caught the eye of a rich relative who owned the field where she happened to glean. It was rather one of those sovereign coincidences, a supernatural intrusion into her life. 📖

Dr. Crabb further explains:

📖 Now God begins to work visibly.... Naomi feels the impact of the young woman's humility and love, and with only a little enthusiasm, smiles weakly and says, "Go ahead, my daughter." That moment is a moment of connecting, where humility and love in one person arouse what little hope remains in another. It is in the community of God's people where God's visible work begins....

Listen to the writer as his pen dances across the pages. "*As it turned out,* she found herself working in a field belonging to Boaz, who was from the clan of Elimelech [Naomi's husband]" (2:3).

I picture the writer pausing after recording that sentence, sitting back and quivering with awe and excitement at the realization that something big is unfolding. Aslan is on the move.

Boaz was God's instrument not merely to solve Naomi's financial problem (though he certainly did that), not only to again fill Naomi's house with the sounds of family (though eventually he did that as well), but to arouse in Naomi a new dream. 📖

In your own life, how have you seen God visibly at work through other people to stimulate your own hope?

How God Deepens Our Desire

9. Listen to Dr. Crabb's further comments on what's happening to Naomi in the events of Ruth 2.

📖 Consider Naomi's words when she heard where Ruth "happened" to work that day. Immediately she recognized the hand of God. "He has not stopped showing his kindness to the living and the dead" (2:20).

Two things require notice. First, the word she used that we translate *kindness* is the Hebrew *hesed.* It's a word that refers to a strongly bonded relationship where one party continues to be faithfully involved with another because it is the character of the first party to do so. Naomi no longer regards Shaddai as a power who could do something but does nothing. Now she sees His kindness, though her family is still dead. God could resurrect them. He hasn't. She continues to view God as kind.

Second, she views that kindness as actually extending to her dead husband and sons, to the "living *and the dead.*" The dream surfacing in Naomi's heart crosses the borders of this world. The better dream that is emerging out of the debris of her already shattered dreams is not just about her, about her life now and her life here. It reaches higher into another world, an unseen one, and at the same time reaches down into the depths of her soul where she discovers what she really wants. 📖

Remember, however, the time frame involved in this development in Naomi's life, as Dr. Crabb points out:

📖 Naomi endured ten years of darkness before God's hand became visible. We're forced to draw an unpleasant and disturbing conclusion: When the pain of shattered dreams helps us discover our desire for God, God seems to disappear. Or at least His absence becomes obvious. And then we feel our desire for God as throbbing agony. We discover how badly we long to know Him. *It is the frustration of our desire for God that deepens it.* Only by *not* revealing God to us, at least for a while—sometimes a long while—can the Spirit put us in touch with a desire that eventually displaces every other desire. 📖

How do you respond to the above observations and conclusions drawn from this part of Naomi's story? Record here your thoughts and impressions:

Addiction—or Deeper Tears

📖 People who find some way to deaden their pain never discover their desire for God in all its fullness. They rather live for relief and become addicts to whatever provides it....

All of us are trapped by addiction to a desire for something less than God. For many women, that something less is relational control. "I will not be hurt again and I will not let people I love be hurt. I'll see to it that what I fear never happens."...

More common in men is an addiction to nonrelational control. "I will experience deep and consuming satisfaction without ever having to relate meaningfully with anyone." 📖

10. In what ways can you relate to any of these indications of "addiction"?

11. Think carefully about the following words:

📖 When dreams shatter, we long to experience God's nearness in a way that dries our tears. Instead, deeper tears are released.

Perhaps that's why so few make any sustained effort to seek God with all their hearts, to discover how deeply they do in fact desire God. The discovery brings pain. We get in touch with a profound desire that we have no power whatsoever to satisfy. We find ourselves at the mercy of One who could provide satisfaction but may not, a Person we cannot manipulate, an unresponsive God who keeps whispering, "Later." The stark truth is a hard one: Discovering our desire for God introduces us to a whole new world of hurt. When we realize how badly we want Him, He seemingly disappears.

But it's a hopeful hurt. It doesn't feel exactly good, but it does feel clean. Through our tears we actually can sing "Great Is Thy Faithfulness" and "It Is Well with My Soul." We can even sing "I Love You, Lord," not without an ache in our hearts but somehow through the ache.

A profound encounter with pain brings us to make a choice. Either we change or we sink into bitterness, despair, or hedonism. Either we accept the fact that life is *not* all about us and how we feel now and what happens here, or we push back the pain by living for the satisfaction of lesser dreams that might come true. 📖

As honestly as you can, describe your own journey in encountering any of the observations and experiences presented in the preceding paragraphs.

Discovering Our Desire for God

12. Dr. Crabb writes, "When we discover our desire for God, we can live for nothing less." How would you evaluate your sincere willingness to come to the point of living for nothing less as you move forward in discovering your desire for God? To what degree is "living for nothing less" an attitude that you truly want to attain?

13. In what ways, if any, are you afraid to reach the point of "living for nothing less"?

📖 But there's a problem, one I've already mentioned. Becoming aware of our desire for God seems to reliably generate severe frustration....

When Shaddai allows terrible pain to come into our lives, He is removing a satisfaction, often a legitimate one like the enjoyment of one's spouse, that keeps us happy and content whether we know God well or not. He is taking away good food to make us hungry for better fare.

But then He doesn't seem to give it. The table stays bare. Those who claim otherwise most often are feeding on their own resources or on their remaining blessings, mistaking them for God....

It is the frustration of our desire for God that deepens it. Only by *not* revealing God to us, at least for a while—sometimes a long while—can the Spirit put us in touch with a desire that eventually displaces every other desire. 📖

14. To what degree have you personally experienced the frustration mentioned above? If you've known this frustration (or know of others who've experienced

it), how would you further describe it? (Remember that strong faith admits when God doesn't seem real; weak faith pretends.)

📖 We will not win the battle against addiction without discovering our desire for God. Therefore, if you want to know God, welcome shattered dreams. Nothing reveals our desire for Him so effectively.

But we must also discover God's desire for us. A *recognized* desire for God exposes our idolatry and sets us on a better path. But only a *fulfilled* desire for God provides the power to consistently resist the lure of lesser pleasures and to stay anchored in Christ when life's storms rage....

How do we experience the reality of God? This is the most important question a Christian can ask....

I'm left wondering: What does it mean for you and me, in this day and age, to experience God? It's one thing to discover our desire for God. It's quite another to discover His desire for us, to know with absolute certainty when life is at its worst that His Presence is real, that He is with us, and that He cares. 📖

15. "How do we experience the reality of God?" Express as fully as you can your present understanding of the answer to this question.

The Elusive God

16. Read carefully through the following extended excerpt from *Shattered Dreams*.

When we discover our desire for God, we're immediately introduced to a new kind of pain. We experience the terrifying dread that we will not find Him.

It was really much easier when we were satisfied with lesser things. One of my happiest friends is a successful businessman with an attractive wife who stays busy with clubs and shopping trips, three kids who are each athletic, bright, and good-looking, and enough money to take the family to the Bahamas for seven days one month and to hunt for a week in Alaska the next. He wonders why I struggle so much. He goes to church. He loves God. He can't figure out why I make Christianity so difficult.

Until we realize how badly we need God, how empty we are without Him, we can sing "Great Is Thy Faithfulness" without worrying whether God really shows up. We can enjoy a happy indifference to whether we discover Him.

For many people, things go well. They feel pretty good. The wonderful truth that God is faithful means to them that He will keep their lives moving along pleasantly. When their path hits a bump, they pray and things get better.

They know God can do something, and He does. Why does God seem to provide so well for the pleasantly committed and to withdraw from the seriously committed? It's enough to make us wonder if we've washed our hands of lukewarm Christianity in vain.

In Exodus, every time the Israelites complained, God blessed them. He straightened things out. Bitter water became sweet, meat and bread rained down from heaven when they told Moses they were hungry. But in Numbers, when they were farther along on their trek to Canaan, God changed tactics. Most often He refused to bless them. When they grumbled about manna, God gave them meat that produced serious indigestion. The next time they fussed about His inadequate provisions, He sent deadly snakes to bite and kill them.

Who wants to become mature? Answered prayer seems to be more frequently reported among younger Christians.

God, it appears, accommodates our immaturity not to keep us there, but to give us a confidence in His Presence that will sustain the search for a deeper, more relational expression of His Presence. The farther we travel on our spiritual journey, the less responsive God becomes to our requests for a pleasant life. Things go wrong and God does nothing. He becomes the elusive God. He is inviting us to an experience with Him that is more fulfilling than an experience with anyone else.

Live long enough and important dreams will shatter. Things will go wrong that God will not fix. He could fix them, but He doesn't.

Then, when the pain of unmet desires puts us in touch with how desperately we long to discover the gentle Presence in our lives, we become more aware of His absence. From deep places in our being that we never knew were there when life was pleasant, we cry out, "God, where are You? Do You care? *Let me find You!*" 📖

What observations or reflections in this quotation can you most identify with, and why?

In what ways can you see that you have experienced the kind of pain spoken of in the above quotation?

Blocking Out the Noise

📖 We must begin our answer by appealing not to experience but to truth. The Bible is clear. God exists. He exists in heaven. He exists on earth. He exists everywhere. Most importantly, He exists *in* us. That's where He is most personally and satisfyingly discoverable.

The life of the Trinity flows in our being (Colossians 2:9-10). Christ is in us (Colossians 1:27). The Spirit has entered us and taken up permanent residence (1 Corinthians 3:16). The Father and Son have made Their home in everyone who loves Jesus, and They promise to let us know They're there (John 14:23).

Our search for God is therefore an *inward* search. Silence and solitude are essential to discovering His Presence. We must block out the noise of life and become aware of our interior world if we're to find God. 📖

17. What does the term "inward search" mean to you—in practical, everyday terms—as you seek to know God?

Look up the Scripture references mentioned in the middle paragraph of the preceding quotation, and view each passage in the fresh light of what you've learned in this workbook. How would you summarize what these passages mean to you in terms of your own experience and responsibility?

📖 If we fail to be quiet enough to hear *all* that the Spirit is saying, we will be in danger of discovering our desire for God and never discovering His desire for us. 📖

18. What does it mean practically for you to "be quiet enough to hear *all* that the Spirit is saying"?

📖 If we're to encounter the divine Presence, we must enter the interior sanctuary of our heart and, like Jesus in the temple, become indignant over what we find. There is no way to God but through the rubble. We must go through, not around, whatever keeps us from Him. The process is what spiritual people call brokenness and repentance.

That does not mean, of course, that we should dwell every minute on what is difficult in our lives....

But we must let our souls live in a private monastery, in an attitude of contemplation that helps us see that all of life is sacred, where we remain alert to the Spirit's revelation of ourselves and God. When life gets tough and God does nothing, the Spirit is telling us that this world is not our home. He is whispering to us about another world and revealing Someone who is faithfully leading us there along the best path. And He is exposing the rubble that must be cleared away. 📖

19. What rubble in your life might need to be exposed and sorted through so you can move forward in the journey of knowing God?

A Bigger Dream

📖 Let me paraphrase Naomi's words when she heard that Ruth had caught the eye of Boaz. "The Lord has not discarded me. He has always been there, but now I can see His kind heart at work. My pain is still real. I've felt it keenly for ten years. But now something matters more. I'm beginning to recognize the shape of a dream that is bigger than every dream I have so far valued." 📖

20. Is this vision of a bigger dream also becoming *your* experience? If so, describe this bigger dream as fully and richly and honestly as you can.

21. In quietness, review what you've written and learned in this week's lesson. If further thoughts or prayer requests come to mind, you may want to write them here.

22. What for you was the most meaningful concept or truth in this week's lesson?

How would you talk this over with God? Write your response here as a prayer to Him.

What do you believe God wants you to do in response to this week's study?

DISCOVERING GOD'S PASSION

THIS WEEK'S LESSON IS BASED ON

CHAPTER 11, "ABANDONMENT AND CONFIDENCE,"

CHAPTER 12, "HIS PASSION RESTRAINED,"

AND CHAPTER 13, "A HELL OF MERCY,"

IN SHATTERED DREAMS BY DR. LARRY CRABB.

O ur journey continues…and Dr. Crabb reminds us that it's something quite different from the life-journey embraced by the secular world and with a much different impact on the traveler's life.

📖 Satan's masterpiece is not the prostitute or the skid-row bum. It is the self-sufficient person who has made life comfortable, who is adjusting well to the world and truly likes living here, a person who dreams of no better place to live, who longs to be only a little better—and a little better off—than he already is.…

The Spirit's masterpiece is the man or woman who much prefers to live elsewhere, who finds no deep joy in the good things of this life, who looks closely in the mirror and yearns to see something different, whose highest dream is to be in the Presence of the grace-filled Father. It is the person whose life *here* is consumed with preparing to meet Him *there*. 📖

As you begin, remember again to ask for the Holy Spirit's help in hearing and obeying His words for you at this time.

Experiencing His Presence

📖 It is possible to meet God. He *does* visit people in this life. We *can* experience His Presence. Self-aware people want nothing more....

More than ever before in my lifetime, people are self-consciously hungry for God, for spiritual renewal, for deep satisfaction of the soul. And we are more in danger than ever before of managing our search and discovering a spirituality without Christ. 📖

1. As you think about what you've learned so far in the *Shattered Dreams Workbook,* what is harmful or wrong about "managing our search" for spiritual renewal?

How can "a spirituality without Christ" masquerade as a spirituality *with* Christ?

What passages of Scripture have helped most to convince you that we *can* experience God's presence in this life?

True Abandonment

📖 The search to discover God requires that we *abandon* ourselves, that we give up control of what matters most, and that we place our *confidence* in Someone we cannot manage. These requirements are as vital as they are difficult....

[T]rue abandonment, giving ourselves to God in utter dependence on His willingness to give Himself to us, pleads only mercy. It allows no room for control. It includes no claim on God that obligates Him to do anything. Only suffering has the power to bring us to this point. 📖

2. On a practical plane, what does this "abandonment" mean to you?

What examples of true abandonment to God have you seen in the lives of other Christians you know? (If you can, include examples of dependence on God not only for material needs, but also for soul needs.)

To truly give ourselves to God, why is it necessary that we trust in His willingness to "give" Himself to us?

In your own soul, how would you describe your understanding and trust of God's willingness to give Himself to you?

3. From a survey of one or more of the following passages, find biblical statements that seem especially to address this topic of abandonment to God. List the significant phrases or verses here, along with any personal comments or questions—such as how the things you've learned in the *Shattered Dreams Workbook* help you view these passages in a different light.

Joshua 1

Psalm 16

Psalm 130

Psalm 131

Proverbs 3

John 14

4. Dr. Crabb states that "only suffering has the power to bring us" to the point of true spiritual abandonment. As you think about what you've learned so far in the *Shattered Dreams Workbook,* explain your understanding of what he means.

True Confidence

📖 Confidence in God…involves an experience that takes us beyond the realm of our five senses. It calls on our capacity to experience spiritual, not material, reality.…

When in the middle of terrible pain we cry out to God, He rarely grants an experience that, with our five senses, we can recognize as God showing up.… But as we abandon ourselves more to Him (What else can we do when we discover that He is all we want?), a confidence emerges, a sense of His Presence, that only the awakened spiritual capacities of the soul can identify. 📖

5. As you consider carefully the preceding quotation, what questions come to your mind? In what respects do you find yourself in strong agreement with these words?

How would you describe or illustrate "the awakened spiritual capacities of the soul" that Dr. Crabb mentions above?

Our Normal Reactions

📖 I wanted to throttle Him…to grab God by the shoulders, shake Him till He paid attention, then tell Him to do a better job of caring for His children.…

I know my reaction is wrong. I know God is God and I'm not.… But sometimes it's hard.…

Throttling God! The image is as ridiculous as it is insubordinate. But what's the alternative? Are we expected to experience God as unresponsive to our well-being and pretend we like Him anyway? Things that matter deeply to us don't seem to matter to Him. What are we to do with that fact? 📖

6. If you can, describe a situation when your own feelings and thoughts were similar to the author's on the occasion he mentions above.

7. Dr. Crabb states that "what many call the Christian life is lifeless surrender to a system they cannot fight, coupled with an attempt to convince themselves they love the Judge." In what ways, if any, have you seen your own tendency to "surrender" in this way?

As you think about what you've learned in the *Shattered Dreams Workbook,* how would such a surrender cause a person to miss out on experiencing God's reality?

Finding Solid Ground

8. As an alternative to such a surrender, Dr. Crabb describes this response: "Scream and holler until the terror of life so weighs you down that you discover solid ground beneath your feet."

And what is this solid ground? He further explains:

📖 The solid ground is not doctrine. It is not merely truth to believe. It is not recommitment and trying harder to believe and do right. It is *Him....*

Solid ground beneath the pain of shattered dreams…is the realization that *it's more difficult for Christ to restrain Himself from making all our dreams come true than for us to watch them shatter.* At our moment of worst pain, Jesus' pain is worse.…

Once our feet touch the solid ground of His passion for us, we can neither dismiss Him as uncaring nor cringe before Him as a ruthless despot. 📖

In an everyday sense, what do you think it means for us to "touch the solid ground of His passion for us"?

9. "Imagine what Jesus must feel," Dr. Crabb writes, "as He stands next to every bed in every hospital. With a word, He could cure every patient. What must He feel as He observes every divorce proceeding in every court?" As you understand the Lord's character, how would you answer this last question?

Dr. Crabb notes that in such a situation Jesus "could do something. Most often He does nothing. The mystery is why." He also states that our awareness of this restraint on the Lord's part can become "not a cause for complaint, but a sacred and appealing mystery." To you, what exactly is "appealing" about this mystery?

10. From a survey of any of the following passages, find convincing evidence of the Lord's "passion to bless." List the significant phrases or verses you see— along with any personal comments or questions, such as how going through the *Shattered Dreams Workbook* helps you view these passages in a different light.

Psalm 145

John 10

Ephesians 1

Revelation 2

Naomi's Story Continues

11. Think about these words as you prepare to read the third chapter of Ruth.

> 📖 Naomi's story offers a powerful illustration of what it means to abandon ourselves to God with confidence that He is there. It's a parable that may help us to depend more completely on God and to discover His desire for us. 📖

After reading Ruth 3, write a concise outline here of the events narrated in that chapter.

12. In the previous chapter of Ruth, we saw Naomi's growing awareness of God's work in her life.

> 📖 But, as is so often the case, when God began to visibly move in Naomi's life, He did not create a smooth path. There was more Naomi needed to learn before she could worship. Through the agony of shattered dreams, her soul was ripped open so she could discover her desire for God. Now she needed to discover God's desire for her. That's what happens next in her story. 📖

In Ruth 3, as "we meet Naomi again," writes Dr. Crabb, "she is a different woman." How so? Near the end of Ruth 3, Dr. Crabb finds another "telling phrase." He had earlier described it this way:

> 📖 If Boaz were to marry Ruth, both Ruth's and Naomi's financial problems would be over. But before he could marry her, Boaz had to overcome a legal hurdle stipulated by Jewish law. The obstacle was real. Ruth may well have been anxious. Would it all work out?

Naomi spoke words of wisdom to Ruth: "Wait, my daughter, until you find out what happens. *For the man will not rest* until the matter is settled today" (3:18). It is true that deliverance comes through a person, but it is also true that the person who delivers us must earnestly long to bring us joy. Deliverance always comes through love....

Naomi has discovered a good man's passion that lets her soul rest and releases her to be powerful in someone else's life. 📖

Dr. Crabb concludes, "In each of our lives...the deliverer is eagerly preparing to bless, unable to rest till He does." Have you sensed this restless, eager-to-bless love from God at this time in your own life? If not, describe any ways in which you may nevertheless be able to trust Him for it.

He Will Not Rest

13. Think about these comments from Dr. Crabb on the significance of this part of Naomi's story (as related in Ruth 3). For each section of commentary below, record your own responses, reflections, and questions in the space provided.

📖 Picture what happened. Boaz, a middle-aged bachelor, wealthy, a devoted follower of Shaddai, wakes up one night at two in the morning and sees a beautiful foreign girl lying at his feet. Perhaps it was her delicate perfume that aroused him. He rubs his eyes, thinking it's a good dream, then looks again. There she is, dressed in alluring clothing and making a clear statement: "I am available to become your wife."

He recognizes her at once as the peasant woman he'd met earlier. Ruth had caught his eye. Boaz had felt immediately drawn, both by her character (he knew of her loyalty to Naomi) and by her youthful beauty. Apparently his tasteful advances to her in the fields had struck a chord. Here she was, cleaned up and pretty, presenting herself to him.

Boaz wanted Ruth. The writer allows no question about that. He wanted to call the rabbi, exchange vows, and take her to bed. If I were writing a steamy novel, I would describe in lurid detail his sexual attraction to Ruth. The description would be accurate. But his passion, though including physical desire, is deeper, richer, more enduringly passionate than fleeting, easily satisfied lust. The inspired writer tells the story of a man who strongly desires a woman. The picture of Christ is hard to miss. 📖

📖 But there's a problem. The law stands between Boaz and Ruth. Jewish law stipulated that the nearest relative had the first right of refusal to marry his relative's widow and assume responsibility for the bereaved family. Boaz was related to Naomi (and so to Ruth), but there was another man more closely related.

Like an honorable lover refusing to enjoy the pleasures of sex until the covenant of marriage was sealed, Boaz withheld himself from Ruth. He actually moved away from her, giving her the noble gift of his absence until he could be with her without dishonor.

Boaz knew the law of the kinsman-redeemer. To marry a relative's widow and restore her to blessing, the candidate must satisfy three criteria. One, he must be a relative, the closest relative willing to assume the role of kinsman-redeemer. Two, he must have the means to pay the entire debt owed by the widow and her family. Three, he must have the power to remove anyone who wanted to remain on the widow's property after all debts were paid.

Ruth, at best vaguely familiar with Jewish law, was aware only that Boaz was withholding himself from her. She must have worried that he didn't really want her. She had discovered her desire for Boaz but was not yet confident of his desire for her. 📖

📖 I picture Naomi sitting on the floor of their little house, warming herself by the fire on a chilly morning. Ruth returns from her night with Boaz, still wearing her prettiest dress but no longer feeling beautiful.

"Naomi, what shall I do? I love Boaz and I think he loves me. But he said he can't marry me until some legal problem is cleared up. Oh, Naomi, I don't know anything about all those technicalities. All I know is that I want him. I don't want anyone else. I want *him.* Doesn't he want me?"

Naomi sits quietly. She knows. Her heart is at rest, quietly thumping with anticipation.

I've often wondered if it occurred to Naomi to suggest Ruth dress in an old rag, work up a sweat, and present herself the next night to the nearest relative. Maybe that would move them through the legal impasse.

Instead, with the wisdom of a spiritual director, she longs for Ruth to *abandon* herself to the heart of one who loves her, with *confidence*—in spite of his restraint—that his desire will find a way to bring them together.

"Ruth," Naomi says, "Boaz wants you more than you want him. He is withholding himself from you for a time at great personal cost. It is harder for him to keep his distance from you than it is for you to wait for him. Know this, that this man will move heaven and earth to find a lawful way to marry you. And that's what you want, a legal marriage that rests on an unshakable foundation. You want nothing less. Wait, my daughter. *The man will not rest* until the matter is settled today." 📖

The Spirit Speaks

14. Dr. Crabb offers the following statements as possible expressions of "the Spirit's words to us." As you're able to accept them in that light—as the Holy Spirit's words to *you*—record your response to each expression in your own words of prayer:

📖 [Y]our Heavenly Bridegroom is consumed with desire for you. 📖

📖 For reasons you cannot now understand, He is holding Himself back from filling your life with every imaginable pleasure. He could do what you're asking Him to do. 📖

📖 When He appears to do nothing, to leave you in your pain and provide no relief, realize this: *The Man will not rest till He makes everything good.* 📖

📖 In the mystery of suffering, enter the deeper mystery of His restrained passion. As the mother holds her baby still so the doctor can deliver the needed injection, so your Lord is allowing you to suffer for reasons you do not know. 📖

📖 Don't try to find comfort in explaining the reasons. Don't try to find the spiritual means to trust more. Enter your pain until your feet touch the solid ground beneath you, the solid ground of the restrained passion of Jesus. 📖

📖 I, the Spirit of Christ, will reveal His passion to you. Create space for Me to fill by waiting, by abandoning yourself to God. When I allow you to discover His desire for you, you will rest with confidence in His love. 📖

📖 Through the pain of shattered dreams, God is awakening us to the possibility of infinite pleasure. That is the nature of our journey; it's what the Spirit is doing. 📖

An Untroubled Heart

15. In the excerpts below, Dr. Crabb elaborates on the potential meaning for us when Jesus says, "Don't let your hearts be troubled." Once more, as you're able to accept these expressions in that light—as words from Jesus to *you*—read them reflectively, then record your prayerful responses to those that speak most to you:

📖 I know things are not now as you want them. I know many of your dreams are not coming true. I want you to understand that things are not as I will one day make them. I like neither the distance between us nor the pain you suffer.... 📖

📖 Until I come to bring you to My Father's house, I am devoting Myself to only one thing: I am preparing a place for you. And My Spirit, on My behalf, is devoting Himself to only one thing— preparing you to enjoy Me and all that I will provide.... 📖

📖 I have called you not to the secular journey where you must make everything in your life now as pleasant as possible. I have called you to the spiritual journey, to a process of enlarging your heart to desire Me above everything else.... 📖

📖 Do not be troubled by all the dreams that will shatter while you remain on earth. You will feel deep pain. But every sorrow you experience will be used by My Spirit to deepen your desire for Me. He will speak to you about Me.... 📖

📖 Listen for the voice. You will hear Him most clearly when suffering humbles you enough to want to hear Him, to know you cannot go on without hearing Him.... 📖

📖 This time of distance, when you will feel such disappointment both with your life and with yourself, will awaken your heart to receive Me with great joy when I finally come. I will not delay. I will come at exactly the appointed time. My Father will give the signal. Listen for the shout.... 📖

16. In quietness, review what you've written and learned in this week's lesson. As further thoughts or prayer requests come to mind, write them here.

17. What for you was the most meaningful concept or truth in this week's lesson?

How would you talk this over with God? Write your response here as a prayer to Him.

What do you believe God wants you to do in response to this week's study?

WANTING SOMETHING BETTER

THIS WEEK'S LESSON IS BASED ON

CHAPTER 14, "A STRANGE WEDDING TOAST,"

CHAPTER 15, "BUT LIFE OUGHT TO WORK,"

AND CHAPTER 16, "IT ISN'T ALWAYS GOOD TO FEEL GOOD,"

IN **SHATTERED DREAMS** BY DR. LARRY CRABB.

W e dive deeper now into a more thorough exploration of themes you've seen earlier in this workbook. As you begin this week's study, ask for God's Spirit to give you genuine insight into these matters.

Naomi's Story Continues

1. Keep the following perspectives in mind as you read the final chapter of the book of Ruth.

   📖 In the last chapter of Naomi's story, we learn two lessons. First, the work of the Spirit will continue through every bump in the road, through every shattered dream. Second, there is one dream God will fulfill for us now, in this life, before we get to heaven, and its fulfillment will bring us joy. 📖

Now write a concise outline of the events narrated in Ruth 4.

A Strange Wedding Toast

2. Dr. Crabb draws our attention in particular to a "strange wedding toast" offered in Ruth 4—the elders' words of blessing upon the marriage of Boaz and Ruth.

> 📖 Here's what the elder said about Ruth: "May the LORD make the woman who is coming into your home like Rachel and Leah, who together built up the house of Israel" (4:11). Was he hoping that Ruth, like Rachel, would be barren and, in her resentment over the shattered dream of bearing children, insist that Boaz have kids through her servant girl? Did he want Ruth to feel unloved, like Leah, and have all the children she could, thinking that one more child might finally win her husband's love?…

Before the elder put down his glass, he added: "Through the off-spring the LORD gives you by this young woman, may your family be like that of Perez, whom Tamar bore to Judah" (4:12). The first part of the toast was strange enough. This addendum is positively bizarre. Was he wishing Ruth to disguise herself as a prostitute to seduce her father-in-law and to bear a child by him? That's what Tamar did. Perez was one of twin boys born to Tamar after she tricked Judah into having sex with her. 📖

What are your own thoughts and reactions to these words of "blessing" spoken for Boaz and Ruth's benefit?

3. Listen now to Dr. Crabb's further comments on this passage. Then record your response to his words plus your further reflections and questions.

📖 "May your wife be like Rachel and Leah." I read that as a toast to brokenness.... I hear the elder telling Boaz something like this: "Boaz, you've married a lovely woman. I want the best for you. But even if the unimaginable happens and Ruth turns out to be as conniving as Rachel or as insecure as Leah, God will still be at work to bring about the good He intends. No matter how bad life may one day make you feel, remember something good is happening that you may not be able to see. Give yourself over to the God who is working out a good plan. Do not settle for rearranging your world merely to feel better. Remember the twelve sons of Israel were born through the likes of Rachel and Leah."

And when the elder added the words, "May your offspring be like Perez whom Tamar bore to Judah," I hear him saying: "Your life might turn into a mess. Trust God to bring good out of whatever happens. Boaz, things will go wrong in your life. Since Eden and until the Second Coming, things have gone wrong and will go wrong in everyone's life. You are immune from no evil. Your failure may trigger even worse failure that will cycle into worse failure still. Look at Judah and Tamar. But their offspring became an ancestor of the Messiah. Give up your demand for blessing that will always help you feel good. When life falls apart, lose all confidence in yourself to put things back together. Yes, I know you're wealthy and powerful. But only God is the author of the truly good. And only the pain of shattered dreams can strip you of confidence in yourself to do anything truly good. Boaz, I wish you brokenness because I wish you joy."

What Our Prayers Reveal

📖 We so easily pray for ourselves and the people we love that we will all be drawn closer to God. I wonder if we know what we're asking. Are we asking to enjoy His blessings with little interest in enjoying His Person?…

When someone shares his story of shattered dreams, our stomachs tighten with fear lest we should meet a similar fate. We dedicate our strongest efforts to helping that person feel better because we're terrified of ever experiencing deep pain that cannot be relieved.

Why? Why do we undervalue intimacy with Christ? Why does the prospect of becoming like Him and close to Him have less appeal than other good things? 📖

4. In your perception, what are the best answers to the "why" questions asked in the last paragraph of the preceding quotation?

📖 The finest things this world can offer have no compelling appeal to a reborn spirit. They are as nothing compared to the joy of living in His Presence.

That's how God sees things. It takes some doing for us to see things the same way. It takes shattered dreams. 📖

5. Here again we see the crucial significance of shattered dreams in preparing us to draw closer to God. What is your reaction to this concept at this time? Do

you fully "buy into" it? Do you have doubts or some other form of resistance to it?

📖 I realize that only in the experience of emptiness does God's Spirit confront us with the choice either to fill ourselves or to abandon ourselves to a God who leaves us empty for a long time and promises fullness later. I have come to believe that suffering is necessary to awaken our desire for God and to develop confidence in His desire for us.

I therefore pray for myself and the people I love that we will experience the severe mercy of shattered dreams, not because I want any of us to hurt but because I long for every one of us to experience the joy of knowing God's love.

I pray that each of our journeys will carry us into seasons of brokenness. 📖

6. How do the words above compare to how you typically pray for your loved ones?

First Things or Second Things?

📖 Society—especially the government but also the church—has taken on the job of producing more untroubled people and fewer seriously troubled people.

Our method has been remarkably consistent: We work hard to improve people's lives, to help people feel good by seeing to it their dreams come true. We devote our energies to improving circumstances—better homes, better families, better jobs—and when bad circumstances cannot be improved, we work to improve people's ability to cope with hard times. We want people, including ourselves, to feel good.

We focus on second things while God is working on first things. 📖

7. What do you think Dr. Crabb most likely means here by "first things" and "second things"?

In your life's most important arenas, how can you join with God in focusing on His "first things" rather than the "second things" we more easily embrace?

📖 It seems we are devoting our best efforts to one central goal: making this life work better so we can feel better. The unchallenged assumption behind our resolve is a delusion. We assume life is *supposed* to work in ways that make us feel the way we want to feel, the way we intuitively and irresistibly sense we were designed to feel.

We further assume that if there is a God, His job is to do what we cannot do to make life work as we want. We conceive of the spiritual journey as a cooperative enterprise where we pool our resources with God's to see to it that life works well enough to keep us relatively happy till we reach the world where life works perfectly and we always feel great. 📖

8. Rightly or wrongly, what have you assumed to be God's "job" in your life?

Counting on God

9. Dr. Crabb notes our tendency to think God should cooperate with us "to make life work so we can feel now all that He has created us to feel." Then he states, "There are two problems with that view":

📖 *One,* better circumstances, whether winning the lottery or saving your marriage, can never produce the joy we were designed to experience. Only an intimate relationship with Perfect Love can provide that joy. *Two,* in this life, we can never feel what God intended us to feel, at least not in full measure. To be completely happy, we must experience perfect intimacy with Perfect Love *and* every "second-thing" blessing that Perfect Love can provide. In this life, we have neither. God will provide both, but not till heaven. 📖

Notice the two *never*s in the preceding quotation. Do you fully agree with the author on these points? Why or why not?

📖 It's hard to hear, but it is important to know that God is *not* committed to supporting our ministries, to preventing our divorces, to preserving our health, to straightening out our kids, to providing a livable income, to ending famine, to protecting us from agonizing problems that generate in our souls an experience that feels like death.

We *cannot* count on God to arrange what happens in our lives in ways that will make us feel good. 📖

10. For you personally, are the preceding statements indeed "hard to hear"? Why or why not?

📖 We *can* count on God to patiently remove all the obstacles to our enjoyment of Him. He is committed to our joy, and we can depend on Him to give us enough of a taste of that joy and enough hope that the best is still ahead to keep us going in spite of how much pain continues to plague our hearts. 📖

11. How exactly do you think we can count on God to "remove all the obstacles to our enjoyment of Him"?

12. What Scripture passages can you think of that relate directly to the main points of the two preceding quotations? How do these passages relate to the points Dr. Crabb is making?

The Spirit's Pull

📖 I know what it is to feel good when life works. For that I make no apology. We should enjoy God's blessings; the good things of life should generate good feelings. But I am coming to see something wrong that before I thought was spiritual gratitude: Those good feelings have become my basis for joy....

I can now feel the powerful undertow within me that has long been pulling me out to sea, into cold waters and uncaring waves. That undertow is an attitude insisting that life continue well enough for me to feel pretty good. When dreams shatter, I then feel alone, unloved, and desperate. And I resolve, more than anything else, to feel better. That resolve is the flesh.

But I can also feel gentle arms around me pulling me toward shore, inviting me to abandon myself to their strength, to believe with confidence that, despite what goes wrong and how bad I feel, they are guiding me toward deep joy. That pull is the Spirit. 📖

13. Think about both the "undertow" and the "gentle arms...pulling me toward shore" as depicted in the preceding quotation. Have you experienced either or both of these impressions? If so, describe those experiences here in your own words.

📖 In this world, the dream of feeling as good as we want to feel *will* shatter.... Shattered dreams will create the opportunity for God to work more deeply than ever before, to further weaken our grasp on our empty selves.

They will also create the opportunity for bitterness and its children, defeat and immorality, to develop. Bitterness carries us farther from shore, into dark nights that never had to be.

Brokenness, on the other hand, allows us to relax in the arms that will bring us to shore, where a warm fire is burning and food has been prepared. 📖

14. In what ways, if any, can you see that God is further weakening your grasp on your empty self?

In what ways have you seen the tendency toward bitterness that this weakening can lead to?

In what ways have you experienced the brokenness that "allows us to relax in the arms that will bring us to shore"?

Flesh and Spirit

15. How would you explain the conflict in our lives between our "flesh" (our sinful nature) and the Spirit, especially as it relates to our experience of shattered dreams?

16. Dr. Crabb includes the following words in "a description of what the Bible calls our *flesh*":

> 📖 Without knowing exactly when it happens, we give up on God—not on His getting us to heaven, but on His making us whole, or at least a little more whole, in this life....
>
> We begin to wonder if we have misread all the promises He made, promises about a peace that passes understanding, promises to anchor our souls with hope and lavish us with joy....
>
> So we take matters into our own hands. We work hard to improve our marriage, to straighten out our kid, to make enough money to pay for the bare necessities. We want things to improve, and now it's clear *why* we want things to improve—we want to feel better. That's our bottom line....
>
> Our misery drives us not to seek God, but to seek to feel better; not to please Him, but to use Him.

We come to a point where there is no more important fact in the world than that we feel bad and there is no deeper desire in our hearts than to feel good....

Look into your heart, study your interior world, and you will find that attitude. It's there in all of us. 📖

Which portions, if any, of the preceding quotation can you especially identify with?

17. Look over 2 Corinthians 4–5 and record your observations of Paul's responses to trouble in his life. How do you think they relate to what you've been learning in this workbook?

A Fork in the Road

18. Dr. Crabb quotes a poem written by Columbine High School student Rachel Joy Scott a few days before she died in the tragic shootings at the school in 1999:

I'm drowning

in my own lake of despair.

I'm choking,

my hands wrapped around my neck.

I'm dying.

Quickly my soul leaves, slowly my

body withers.

It isn't suicide,

I consider it homicide.

The world you created has led to my death.*

Dr. Crabb then asks, "Suppose you had been a trusted confidante to Rachel, someone whom she asked to read her poem. What might you have said after reading it? More important, what view of life would have determined your response?"

He then suggests what we *might* say in such a situation if we more fully understood God's ways. As you read through each paragraph of this suggested response, think about your own life's journey and that of people close to you, especially anyone who might be hurting at this time. Choose one or more of the paragraphs to reflect upon, and record your thoughts and questions in the space provided.

📖 Rachel, your pain is legitimate. You've discovered the part of your soul that longs for what this world will never provide. Your integrity has burdened you with the severe mercy of realizing that nothing in this world provides true joy. 📖

---

* Rachel Joy Scott, quoted by Richard Roeper, "One year later, Columbine still offers no easy answers," *Denver Post*, 20 April 2000, sec. B, p. 9.

📖 You've come to a fork in the road. One path beckons you with the promise that life can work well, and God exists to see to it that things go well enough for you to feel pretty good. 📖

📖 The other path, the narrow one that not many choose, invites you to live in a disappointing world where good dreams will shatter and you will sometimes feel empty and alone, sometimes so empty and alone that it will seem like death. But this path promises the eventual discovery of a consuming desire within you for God and, far better, the thrilling discovery of His consuming desire to be intimate with you. 📖

📖 After many dark nights, you will taste the joy of that intimacy. You will not be able to describe it, but you will feel alive, hopeful, solid, even in the middle of continued anguish over hard circumstances. 📖

📖 Abandon yourself to God. He will seem at times cruelly unresponsive, callously indifferent. You will be tempted to manage life on your own, to do whatever you can to feel better. 📖

📖 But if you're quiet, you will hear both His voice and yours leading you to the narrow path. 📖

19. In quietness, review what you've written and learned in this week's lesson. As further thoughts or prayer requests come to mind, record them here.

20. What for you was the most meaningful concept or truth in this week's lesson?

How would you talk this over with God? Write your response here as a prayer to Him.

What do you believe God wants you to do in response to this week's study?

THE BEST DREAM

THIS WEEK'S LESSON IS BASED ON

CHAPTER 17, "THE THREE LESSONS OF BROKENNESS,"

CHAPTER 18, "OUR HIGHEST DREAM—IF WE ONLY KNEW IT,"

AND CHAPTER 19, "A DREAM COME TRUE,"

IN **SHATTERED DREAMS** BY DR. LARRY CRABB.

A s you begin, ask for the Holy Spirit's help in hearing and obeying His words for you at this time, with these words from Dr. Crabb in mind:

📖 May I suggest that you set this book aside for a few minutes and pray. If your heart feels chilly and uninvolved, ask the Spirit to make you aware of a hunger for Christ that is stronger than your hunger for anything else. 📖

1. If you would like to, write here a prayer such as the author suggests.

Naomi's Story Continues

2. Read again the final scenes of Naomi's story as recorded in Ruth 4:13-22. What impresses you most about Naomi in these scenes?

3. "Naomi's story ends with her feeling passion for God," writes Dr. Crabb.

> 📖 She's no longer resentful, depressed, and empty, but quiet, joyful, and aware of more than she could see. This last episode of her life is recorded by the Spirit, I believe, to help us see the path to joy and to draw us to join Naomi on the journey.
>
> The book of Ruth ends with a simple scene. Picture yourself in the theater. The curtain rises for the last act. The stage is barren except for a rocking chair. A wrinkled but peaceful-looking old woman sits on that chair, holding a month-old boy on her lap. We watch as she looks down into the innocent eyes of the child with her eyes of love. Then, slowly, she lifts her gaze to heaven. She says nothing. It's as if we aren't there. No one is there. Naomi is in the Presence of God. We hear a chorus of women's voices sing, "Naomi has a son." She continues holding him on her lap, looking up. The curtain drops. And we sit....
>
> She's now an old lady. Her first grandson has just been born. She remains a widow. Elimelech is not with her to share her joy. Her son is absent. The child's father should be Mahlon. Instead it is Boaz, a kind relative but not Naomi's son. So many of her dreams are still

shattered. God has done nothing to restore them. But He has surfaced a higher dream and is right now fulfilling that dream as Naomi holds Obed on her lap. 📖

Record here your own responses to this description and commentary plus any further reflections and questions of your own.

On Her Lap

4. In this last portion of the book of Ruth, Dr. Crabb finds a final "telling phrase" that further shows how God has brought Naomi along on her journey to joy. The phrase is "on her lap" (4:16).

    It's a phrase that "suggests her participation in a much greater dream," he explains. However, we won't catch the excitement of Naomi's dream "unless we set it squarely against the backdrop of human misery. Bear with me as I arrange the set where Naomi is sitting."

    Dr. Crabb "arranges the set" by describing the biblical significance of the phrase *on her lap*. Read carefully the scriptural background he offers below.

    📖 The specific phrase "on her lap" occurs three times elsewhere in the Bible, all in Genesis. A brief look at those instances will reveal the climax to Naomi's story hidden in this final scene.

    First, Rachel, Jacob's wife, is barren and none too happy about it. She demands that Jacob sleep with her servant girl so that when a baby is born, Rachel can hold it on her lap. "Sleep with her," she instructs Jacob, "so that she can bear children *for me*"—literally, "on my lap" (Genesis 30:3)....

Rachel longed to be part of God's story but wouldn't trust God to make it happen. In the pain of her shattered dreams, she took control....

Second, Jacob, now an old man, can barely see. Just before he dies, he holds his two grandsons Ephraim and Manasseh (Joseph's sons) on his lap. He turns to Joseph and says, "I never expected to see your face again, and now God has allowed me to see your children too" (48:11). In the next verse, the boys are lifted from Jacob's *knees*—literally, from his lap....

Jacob saw his highest dream realized in watching God move through his life and on through others to continue the journey to joy. When he saw not only his long absent son but also his son's children, he rested in the joy of knowing God was continuing to do him good....

Third, Joseph is in Egypt, years later. He longs to be in the Promised Land, but faces death in Egypt. We're told that by now he has seen "the third generation of Ephraim's children. Also the children of Makir son of Manasseh were placed at birth on Joseph's knees," literally, on his lap (50:23). With the children on his lap, he speaks his final words to his family: "I am about to die. But God will surely come to your aid and take you up out of the land to the land he promised." Then he adds, "And then you must carry my bones up from this place" (50:24-25). Joseph doesn't want to miss the party he knows is coming, a party that death would not prevent him from enjoying.

Joseph realized that his death was not an ending but rather another chapter in a story that would end well. 📖

With this biblical background in mind, how would you explain in your own words the significance of the phrase "on her lap" in Naomi's story?

5. "And now Naomi, as her life ends, is holding her grandson *on her lap,*" writes Dr. Crabb. "After her journey through shattered dreams, I hear this prayer flowing from her heart:"

📖 "O God, the path has been rough. I miss my husband. I miss my sons. The pain is still real. But you have given me a sense of Your Presence and the certainty that You have called me to be part of Your sovereign plan.

"And I am tasting community as never before. Ruth is a wonderful young woman, Boaz is a good man, and this baby—well, I've never seen anything so beautiful. This is spiritual community, a community of people through whom You are working toward a higher purpose.

"God, I am not now who I used to be. I was depressed, angry, and afraid of the future. Now I am content, grateful, and full of joy knowing You are here and You are moving. I am a transformed woman. My pain continues, but I'm anchored in hope." 📖

Record below your own response to this imagined prayer of Naomi's. How much can you identify in your own life with these words?

Lessons of Brokenness

In chapter 17 of *Shattered Dreams,* Dr. Crabb points us to "three lessons of bro-kenness." Reflect on these as you see them summarized in the next few pages.

6. The first lesson:

> 📖 The good news of the gospel is not that God will provide a way to
> make life easier. The good news of the gospel, for this life, is that He
> will make our lives better. We will be empowered to draw close to
> God and to love others well and to do both for one central purpose,
> to glorify God, to make Him look good to any who watch us live....
>
> The journey to God will always, at some point, take us through
> darkness where life makes no sense. Life isn't easy; it's hard, some-
> times very hard. 📖

Which thoughts and phrases in the preceding "lesson" carry the most weight
for you?

How would you restate this lesson in a way that has the most personal application to you at this time?

7. The second lesson:

📖 When God seems most absent from us, He is doing His most important work in us....

The felt absence of God is a gift to gratefully receive. During those seasons of darkness He is doing His deepest work in us. 📖

In this "lesson," which thoughts or phrases carry the most weight for you?

How would you restate this lesson in a way that has the most personal application to you at this time?

8. The third lesson:

📖 It isn't always good to be blessed with the good things of life. Bad times provide an opportunity to know God that blessings can never provide....

Feeling good is not the goal. When we feel bad, we have the opportunity to do battle against the enemy within that keeps us from entering the Presence of God with no greater passion than to glorify Him. 📖

Once more, which thoughts or phrases in this "lesson" carry the most weight for you?

And how would you restate this lesson in a way that is most personally applicable to you at this time?

Looking to Jesus

📖 True obedience to Christ springs from a deep passion for Christ. But where does the passion come from? How do we get it? 📖

9. To your best spiritual understanding at this time, how would you answer the questions in the preceding quotation?

📖 We look up. We see Jesus. He is screaming, hanging on a cross....

We keep looking, and we listen. We hear God declare, "It is enough!" We hear Jesus cry, "It is finished!" We hear the Spirit whisper to us, "Look now into the face of God. The veil covering His glory is removed. See Him and live!"

We see a smile. We hear a song. We realize, as if for the first time (though we've been Christians for years), that our deepest need, our deepest desire, is *not* for relief from current troubles. We don't even deserve relief.

Our deepest desire is for a kind of life only mercy makes possible, a life only grace provides. It is for life from God, life with God, life for God.

And we have it. We've had it since the day we trusted Christ to forgive our sins. But it took shattered dreams to put us more deeply in touch with what we already have. The pain carried us into depths of our heart that are still ugly, but the Spirit took us deeper, into the very core of our being, where Christ lives, where we are alive. 📖

10. With the preceding thoughts in mind, allow the Holy Spirit's voice to speak through any of the following passages, helping you look up and see Jesus. Feel free to write your prayerful responses in the space below.

Hebrews 2:9

Hebrews 9:28

Hebrews 12:2-3

Hebrews 13:20-21

1 Peter 2:22-25

1 John 4:10

Revelation 5:4-10

First-Order Hope

📖 I realize the very best thing I can do for my newborn grandson is to be a grandfather who delights in the pleasures of God. Maybe the passion coming out of my soul for God will give him the courage to face his own deepest yearnings with hope that more than his stomach can be filled.

My eyes turn away from his. I look up. Tears blur my vision enough to see the face of God.

My heart swells with worship. I discover again how deeply my soul pants for God. Encounter with God, not holding my grandson, defines life. And because I know that, I long for God to reveal Himself to Jake, even if it requires shattered dreams to make it happen.

I still hope Jake stays healthy, does well in school, has lots of friends, meets a nice girl, marries, fathers beautiful kids, and leads his family into meaningful involvement with a local church. But those are all second-order hopes. My first-order hope for Jake is that he encounter God. 📖

11. As you think about these thoughts from the author toward his grandson, how would you express your highest longings for those you love most?

A Prayer in the Darkness

12. Dr. Crabb offers the following prayer as an expression that comes "in the middle of a dark night that has revealed the Son within us." Listen sensitively to these words. Choose one or more of the statements to reflect upon, and record your prayerful responses in the space provided.

> 📖 Lord, I can feel within me the demand that You be a better friend. 📖

> 📖 I can sense my almost irresistible urge to turn to sources of pleasure that provide the relief You withhold. There are many. Some are people—my spouse, my kids, my counselor, my golf buddies. Others are activities like sex and busyness, or things like money and competence. 📖

📖 But none provides life. Only You, on Your terms, can satisfy my soul. 📖

📖 At this moment, though, I don't feel satisfied. I feel empty, desperate, alone. If I believed that there was a better friend than You, I would turn from You. 📖

📖 But I see the cross. I see Your holy wrath and my blaspheming arrogance and I know I deserve not relief but eternal misery. I deserve the emptiness of eternity without love or meaning. And I see Jesus bearing Your wrath so I can receive Your eternal kindness. I have no other friend like that. 📖

📖 How can I turn to anyone else? It would be insanity, foolishness. You are God. I am not. I abandon myself to You. 📖

📖 Like Jabez, I ask that you bless me. I ask that you satisfy the highest dream my heart can envision—an encounter with You. 📖

Learning from Naomi's Story

13. Early in the book *Shattered Dreams,* Dr. Crabb pointed to "one central lesson that Naomi's story teaches":

📖 Shattered dreams open the door to better dreams, dreams that we do not properly value until the dreams that we improperly value are destroyed. Shattered dreams destroy false expectations, such as the "victorious" Christian life with no real struggle or failure. They help us discover true hope. We need the help of shattered dreams to put us in touch with what we most long for, to create a felt appetite for better dreams. And living for the better dreams generates a new, unfamiliar feeling that we eventually recognize as joy. 📖

Below are a few phrases taken from the summary above. Think about how each phrase corresponds to something in your own life at this time. If something comes to mind, write it down. (To some degree you may be repeating answers you've given to earlier questions, but this repetition can help deepen your grasp of the lessons God is now teaching you.)

a. "better dreams"

b. "dreams that we improperly value"

c. "false expectations"

d. "true hope"

e. "what we most long for"

14. In quietness, review what you've written and learned in this week's lesson. Record here any further thoughts or prayer requests as they come to mind.

15. What for you was the most meaningful concept or truth in this week's lesson?

    How would you talk this over with God? Write your response here as a prayer to Him.

    What do you believe God wants you to do in response to this week's study?

TRULY EXPERIENCING GOD

THIS WEEK'S LESSON IS BASED ON

CHAPTER 20, "THERE'S A NEW WAY TO LIVE—AND IT'S POSSIBLE,"

AND CHAPTER 21, "THE JOURNEY TO JOY,"

IN **SHATTERED DREAMS** BY DR. LARRY CRABB.

In our concluding lesson, remember once more to ask for the Holy Spirit's help in hearing and obeying His words for you at this time.

The Exact Center

1. Read this excerpt from *Shattered Dreams,* as Dr. Crabb builds to a statement concerning Christianity's "exact center."

   📖 For years we've presented Christianity as little more than a means of escaping hell. Knowing Jesus has been reduced to a one-time decision that guarantees the chance to live in a perfect, pain-free world forever.

   Christianity is about going to heaven, but that's not the center of Jesus' kindness to us.

Nor is it the opportunity to lead fulfilled, meaningful lives now. Returning to our Maker's manual and following biblical principles to make our marriages work and our kids turn out well and our bank accounts comfortably bulge is not God's plan for our lives....

Jesus revealed His highest dream for all His followers when in prayer He defined the true abundant life in these words: "that they may know you, the only true God, and Jesus Christ, whom you have sent" (John 17:3).

The exact center of Christianity is the opportunity it provides to enjoy God, to be more satisfied with Him than with anyone or anything else. 📖

Based on what you know of Scripture, how fully do you agree with this identification of Christianity's "exact center"?

What difference do you think it could make—and should make—when the true understanding of this "exact center" is embraced in your personal life?

What difference could it make as this "exact center" is embraced by your church?

Only Suffering

📖 If Luther is right—that only in suffering do we learn to fully delight in God's goodness—then it becomes immediately clear why our enjoyment of God is so shallow. We don't like to suffer. We see no value in suffering. We arrange our lives to minimize suffering. And we believe Christianity offers a God who will cooperate with that plan. 📖

2. What value in suffering do you honestly see and appreciate?

3. Review some of the following familiar passages in a fresh way, in light of your thoughts and discoveries while going through the *Shattered Dreams Workbook*. How do these biblical teachings relate to your perspectives on suffering and life's hardships? In what ways do you view these passages differently than before?

Psalm 119:67,68,71,75

Romans 5:3

2 Corinthians 4:16-18

Philippians 1:29-30

Hebrews 12:7-11

James 1:2-4

📖 So the question we must squarely face is this: Does knowing God really provide the pleasure our souls were designed to enjoy? Can we enjoy God more than anyone or anything else? Is it possible? 📖

4. What, more than anything else, convinces you that the answer to the above questions is "Yes"?

Only Worship

📖 The cure…for every form of slavery to something other than God is worship. Not the dull worship of rote routine or the shallow worship of contrived excitement, but worship that creates deep pleasure in the One who receives it and the one who gives it.

Only a thrilling, soul-pleasuring encounter with God that generates more pleasure than sin will free us from our addiction to sin. 📖

5. As you worship God, privately or with others, what do you seek most to know or experience? Express this longing in words as fully as you can, perhaps in the form of a prayerful plea to God your Father.

Your Journey to Joy

6. Mark or highlight any of the phrases in the quotation below that most strongly reflect your own genuine longings at this time.

📖 Perhaps you're aware of how badly you long to experience God. Many dreams have shattered in your life, important ones, but you don't want to dishonor God. You don't want to dismiss Him. You desire to know Christ as your best friend.

You want to enjoy Him and know His power to relate well with others, to be a better friend, to parent your children more wisely, to touch hurting people more deeply.

And you want to change, to find the strength to resist sinful urges, to persevere in your difficult marriage, to replace self-hatred and despair with an awareness of your unique value in the kingdom of Christ.

You long for an encounter with God, community with others, and real transformation within your self....

[Y]ou want to encounter *God,* to find in your relationship with Him a pleasure that exceeds all other pleasures, a joy that sustains you in every sorrow. 📖

Where do you think these desires come from? Why are they within you?

How Do You Think About God?

In the final chapter of *Shattered Dreams,* Dr. Crabb puts before us two core questions. The first is, "How do you think about God?" He points out three basic answers.

7. The first answer:

📖 The Bible reveals God as absolutely holy. The angels who continually surround Him cry out, "Holy, holy, holy is the Lord God Almighty."

Paul introduces God to us in Romans as a holy God who is passionately furious at all that is unholy. His presentation of the good news of the gospel starts with bad news for us. God is a God of vengeance, of wrath, of retribution. He will not allow the guilty to remain unpunished. The picture is not one of a nice man; He is not presented as a warm and loving father who likes His children and who sees to it they all have a good time. 📖

What aspects of this description, if any, match closely your own perspective of God?

8. The second answer:

> 📖 Our Christian culture has weakened our understanding of the holiness of God by introducing too soon the idea of grace....
>
> God means for us to obey His rules, we say, but if we don't (and no one does, of course, not completely), He's really quite understanding. That's our view of grace....
>
> We reduce the holy God of passionate wrath to a fatherly God with strict standards. And we do it in the name of grace. 📖

What aspects of this description, if any, match closely your own perspective of God?

9. The third answer:

📖 But we're still uncomfortable with the idea of standards. It restricts our freedom; it denies us the chance to be ourselves, to express who we really are. So we dismiss God's standards by attacking them as holdovers from legalism. God is the God of liberty. We're told to stand fast in the freedom Christ provides.

That freedom, we say, consists in our opportunity to find ourselves and become whole persons by following God's wise counsel, by listening to our inner voice. In His kindness, God has given us a lot of ideas about how to live. If we listen to them and practice them, we'll enjoy life as it was meant to be enjoyed. Things will go well for us. We'll feel good about ourselves and how our lives are turning out.

God has now become the helpful God of useful principles. 📖

Once more, what aspects of this description, if any, match closely your own perspective of God?

How Do You Think About Yourself?

The second core question the author asks in the final chapter of *Shattered Dreams* is this: "How do you think about yourself?" Again he offers three potential answers to this question.

10. The first answer:

📖 If you're looking for a quick boost to your self-esteem, the Bible is not a good book to read. You might especially want to skip the first three chapters of Romans. They reveal us as hopelessly arrogant, foolish enough to think that we're the point of things, that our happiness, our sense of well-being, matters more than anything else. 📖

What aspects of this description, if any, match closely the way you view yourself?

11. The second answer:

📖 In our Christian culture, we've weakened our understanding of personal sin by talking too soon and too much about our longings and our needs. We want to feel good about ourselves, we long for enjoyable relationships, we desire effective and recognized ministries. *We* become the point and see nothing really wrong with it.

Because we focus more on our longings than our evil, we see ourselves not as hopelessly arrogant, worthy of eternal misery, but as scoldably selfish, deserving of perhaps a slap on the wrist....

We've weakened our view of sin by centering on what we long for to the point where, at worst, we see ourselves as deserving only a scolding. 📖

What aspects of this description, if any, match closely your view of yourself?

12. The third answer:

> 📖 We take it one step further. We may admit that our minor offenses warrant a reprimand, but we really believe that if someone knew what we've been through and the pain we feel, the scolding would give way to a sympathetic hug. We struggle and we make mistakes, but given our hurt, given how poorly the people in our lives have responded to our longings, our struggles are quite understandable. If God loves us, He really ought to help. 📖

Again, what aspects of this description, if any, match closely your own self-view?

Encountering God

Dr. Crabb then brings together, in various ways, these basic views we have of God and of ourselves and shows what happens.

13. First:

> When understandable strugglers meet a helpful God of useful
> principles, they use Him to make their lives more comfortable. They
> never encounter God as their greatest pleasure, they never enter into
> an other-centered community of broken people, and they never
> experience a deep change in their interior being. Their experience of
> God is shallow.
>
> They become spiritual narcissists, nutty people who live only to
> feel better.

In what ways, if any, does this description reflect your own experiences, past
or present?

14. Second:

> When scoldably selfish people meet a fatherly God of strict stan-
> dards, their encounter with God is never intimate. It breeds resent-
> ment and distance. They, too, never encounter God as their greatest
> pleasure. Their approach to community becomes appropriate and
> well-mannered, and they turn into self-righteous Pharisees who con-
> gratulate themselves on being better than others.
>
> They become spiritual hypocrites, nutty people who think of
> themselves as quite mature.

In what ways, if any, does this description reflect your own experiences, past or present?

15. Third:

> 📖 But when arrogant people who know they deserve eternal misery tremble before a holy God of passionate wrath, they discover grace. They encounter the depths of God's kindness and love, a kindness and love they find nowhere else. They fall to their knees and worship Christ as their Lord and Savior and as their truest friend, really their only true friend. They know they don't *deserve* a hug, no matter how badly they're hurting; but they get an eternal one anyway. That's the grace that takes their breath away. 📖

Once more, in what ways, if any, does this third description reflect your own experiences, past or present?

In what ways does this third description reflect your longings for the *future*?

Those Who Truly Understand

16. In the final pages of *Shattered Dreams,* Dr. Crabb provides the following further description of people who deeply understand the true biblical view of God and themselves. As you've done before, read these words reflectively, choose one or more of the paragraphs to reflect upon, then record your prayerful responses in the space provided. How fully do these statements describe you?

   📖 They enter into the community of broken, forgiven people who are hungry for all of God they can get. Nothing stands in their way—not shame, not the fear of revealing too much, not a desire to be well thought of. With abandon they seek God, alone and in the company of like-minded others. 📖

   📖 They're startled when they discover that their interior worlds are changing. They discover that they actually *want* to obey God. They find themselves caring less about their own reputation than about God's. 📖

📖 They become spiritual people, not nutty but wise as they dream the dream of knowing Christ even better. 📖

📖 And they welcome shattered dreams as friends. They enter their pain and discover an arrogant spirit that says, "I don't deserve this." They tremble in their unholiness before a holy God and discover how passionately they want to have a good relationship with Him. Then He reveals the new way of grace, the gospel that lets them draw near to God and discover how wonderful He is. 📖

x

y

z

w

v

u

t

s

r

q

p

o

n

m

l

k

j

i

h

g

f

e

d

c

b

a

📖 But they learn slowly. More dreams must shatter before they experience their deepest joy in Christ. 📖

📖 The journey continues, a journey through shattered dreams to the exquisite joy of encountering Christ. 📖

A New Way

📖 A new way to live is available to us, a way that leads to a joy-filled encounter with Christ, to a life-arousing community with others, and to a powerful transformation of our interior worlds that makes us more like Jesus....

I am praying for a revolution in the church of Jesus Christ, a revolution that takes full advantage of the new way of the Spirit....

Pray with me that many will walk together in the new way, that the revolution will begin. We can live beyond shattered dreams. 📖

17. Will you join the author in this prayer? If so, you may want to record here your genuine expression of this request before God.

18. In quietness, review what you've written and learned in this week's lesson. Record here any further thoughts or prayer requests as they come to mind.

19. What for you was the most meaningful concept or truth in this week's lesson?

    How would you talk this over with God? Write your response here as a prayer to Him.

    What do you believe God wants you to do in response to this week's study?

THE PARABLE

"What's the world's greatest lie?" the boy asked.
"It's this: that at a certain point in our lives,
we lose control of what's happening to us,
and our lives become controlled by fate.
That's the world's greatest lie."

—PAULO COELHO

The man's life was pleasant. So too was his worship. The two always go together.

God was not pleased. So He allowed the man's life to become unpleasant.

The man responded at once with shock. "How can this be? How could this happen in my life?"

Beneath the shock, the man was smug. But he could not see it. He thought it was trust. "This will soon pass. God is faithful. Life will again be pleasant." His worship remained shallow.

God was not pleased. So He allowed more unpleasant things to happen in the man's life.

The man tried hard to handle his frustrations well, like someone who trusted God. "I will be patient," he resolved.

But he didn't notice that his efforts to be patient grew out of the conviction that a pleasant life was his due. He did not hear his own heart saying, "If I'm patient, God will make things pleasant again. That's His job."

His worship became a way to convince God to restore his pleasant life.

God was not pleased. So He pulled back His hedge of protection around the man a little farther. The man's life became miserable.

The man got angry. God seemed unmoved, indifferent, uncaring. Heaven's door slammed shut. The man knew he could not pry it open.

He could think only of better days—not of better days coming, but of better days before, days that no longer were and that showed no signs of returning.

His highest dreams were a return to those days, to the pleasant life he once knew, when he felt what he had called joy.

He could not imagine a higher dream than going backward to what once was. But he knew life never moved backward. Adults never become children again. Old people never recover the energy of their most productive years.

So he lost hope. God had withdrawn His blessing, and there was no indication He would change His mind.

The man fell into depression. His worship stopped.

God was not pleased. So He released the forces of hell into the man's life.

Temptations that formerly were manageable now became irresistible. The pain of living was so great that the pleasure the temptations afforded, relief really, seemed reasonable and necessary. But after the pleasure came a new kind of pain, a kind of pain that covered his soul with a fog that not even the brightest sun could penetrate.

The man could see only his pain. He could not see God. He thought he could, but the god he saw was one whose job it was to relieve pain. He could imagine this god, but he could not find him.

He addressed the only god he knew. He begged for help. Beneath his words of pleading he could almost hear what his heart was saying: "You *owe* me help. I will never believe I deserved all this to happen. This pain is not my fault. It's yours."

His worship had always been a demand, but now the demand was so obvious the man could almost recognize it.

God was not pleased. So He let the struggles continue. And God allowed new troubles to come into the man's life.

In the part of the man's heart that dreamed his greatest dreams, he had been certain he would never have to face these new troubles that were now in his life. For years he had said in his heart (without actually hearing it), "*That* could never happen to me. If it did, my life would be over. If *that* happened, I'd have no choice but to conclude that God isn't good. I would have to dismiss God. And no one, not even God, could fault me."

But still the man could not hear his heart speak. What he could hear was a seductive voice that made the worst temptation he had ever faced—to lose hope in God—seem noble, bravely defiant, the only way left for the man to find himself.

The battle waxed hot. But a flicker of hope remained. The man held on to his faith. Even as he did, he could not hear his heart saying, "I have every right to give up on my faith. But I'm choosing the truly noble way. I still believe in You. I still believe You're there and that my highest hopes for joy—whatever hopes are left—lie with you. Does *that* impress you? If not, my God, what does?"

His worship was more desperate than ever. But it was still proud.

God was not pleased. So He allowed the man's trials to continue and his pain to remain unabated. God kept His distance from the man. He provided no comfort, no tangible reason to hope. It was difficult for God not to make everything better in the man's life. It was even more difficult for Him not to appear directly to the man and assure him of His presence.

But He didn't. God had a greater dream for the man than a return to a pleasant life. He wanted the man to find true joy. He longed to restore the man's hope for what mattered most. But still the man did not know what that was.

The fog around the man's soul thickened until he could feel it, like walls closing in. All that was left was mystery; there was fear certainly, even terror, but more acute was the sense of mystery, the mystery of a bad life and a good God.

Where *was* He? When the man became most aware of his need for God, God disappeared. It made no sense. Was God there or not? If He was, did He care? Or didn't He?

The man could not give up on God. He remembered Jacob. So he began to fight. But he fought in the dark, a darkness so deep that he could no longer see his dreams of a pleasant life.

In deep darkness, you cannot see. But you can hear. He could hear for the first time what his heart was saying.

"Bless me!" he cried. From his deepest soul, he could hear words reflecting a resolve that would not let go of God.

"Bless me! Not because I am good, but because You are good. Bless me! Not because I deserve Your blessing, but because it is Your nature to bless. You really can't help Yourself. I appeal not to who I am. You owe me nothing. I appeal only to who You are."

He still saw his pain. But now he saw God. And the cry for blessing was no longer a demand for a pleasant life. It was a cry for whatever God wanted to do, for whoever He was. The man felt something different. It was the beginning of humility. But the very fact of what it was kept him from seeing what it was.

The man had forgotten himself and discovered his desire for God. He did not find God right away, but he had hope, hope that he might experience what his soul most deeply longed for.

Then he saw it. Fresh water bubbled up from a spring in the desert of his soul, and he saw it. It was a new dream. He could see its contours take shape. It was a dream of actually knowing God and representing Him in an unpleasant world. The dream took on a specific focus; he saw how he could know God and represent God to others in a way that was *his* way and not someone else's. It felt like coming home.

He realized immediately that his power to speak on behalf of God to others in the midst of their unpleasant lives depended on his speaking from the midst of his own unpleasantness. He had never before felt grateful for his troubles.

His suffering became to him a doorway into God's heart. He shared God's pain in His great project of redemption. Suffering together for a single cause made him feel closer to God.

A new thought occurred to him. "I will join with whatever forces are opposed to the root of this unpleasantness. I will ally with goodness against evil. I will not wait to see more clearly; what my hand finds to do, I will do. But I will stay close to the spring. My soul is thirsty. A pleasant life is not water for my soul; whatever comes from God—whoever God is—this is the only true water. And it is enough."

The man worshiped God, and God was pleased. So God kept the water bubbling up out of the spring in the man's soul. When the man didn't drink every morning from that spring or return every evening to drink again, his thirst became intolerable.

Some things in his life got better. Some things stayed the same. Some things got worse.

But the man was dreaming new dreams, greater dreams than a pleasant life. And he found the courage to pursue them. He was now a man with hope, and his hope brought joy.

God was very pleased. So was the man. 📖

THE BOOK OF RUTH

Chapter 1

¹In the days when the judges ruled, there was a famine in the land, and a man from Bethlehem in Judah, together with his wife and two sons, went to live for a while in the country of Moab. ²The man's name was Elimelech, his wife's name Naomi, and the names of his two sons were Mahlon and Kilion. They were Ephrathites from Bethlehem, Judah. And they went to Moab and lived there.

³Now Elimelech, Naomi's husband, died, and she was left with her two sons. ⁴They married Moabite women, one named Orpah and the other Ruth. After they had lived there about ten years, ⁵both Mahlon and Kilion also died, and Naomi was left without her two sons and her husband.

⁶When she heard in Moab that the LORD had come to the aid of his people by providing food for them, Naomi and her daughters-in-law prepared to return home from there. ⁷With her two daughters-in-law she left the place where she had been living and set out on the road that would take them back to the land of Judah.

⁸Then Naomi said to her two daughters-in-law, "Go back, each of you, to your mother's home. May the LORD show kindness to you, as you have shown to your dead and to me. ⁹May the LORD grant that each of you will find rest in the home of another husband."

Then she kissed them and they wept aloud ¹⁰and said to her, "We will go back with you to your people."

¹¹But Naomi said, "Return home, my daughters. Why would you come with me? Am I going to have any more sons, who could become your husbands? ¹²Return home, my daughters; I am too old to have another husband. Even if I thought there was still hope for me—even if I had a husband tonight and then gave birth to sons—¹³would you wait until they grew up? Would you remain unmarried for them? No, my daughters. It is more bitter for me than for you, because the LORD's hand has gone out against me!"

¹⁴At this they wept again. Then Orpah kissed her mother-in-law good-by, but Ruth clung to her.

¹⁵"Look," said Naomi, "your sister-in-law is going back to her people and her gods. Go back with her."

[16]But Ruth replied, "Don't urge me to leave you or to turn back from you. Where you go I will go, and where you stay I will stay. Your people will be my people and your God my God. [17]Where you die I will die, and there I will be buried. May the LORD deal with me, be it ever so severely, if anything but death separates you and me." [18]When Naomi realized that Ruth was determined to go with her, she stopped urging her.

[19]So the two women went on until they came to Bethlehem. When they arrived in Bethlehem, the whole town was stirred because of them, and the women exclaimed, "Can this be Naomi?"

[20]"Don't call me Naomi," she told them. "Call me Mara, because the Almighty has made my life very bitter. [21]I went away full, but the LORD has brought me back empty. Why call me Naomi? The LORD has afflicted me; the Almighty has brought misfortune upon me."

[22]So Naomi returned from Moab accompanied by Ruth the Moabitess, her daughter-in-law, arriving in Bethlehem as the barley harvest was beginning.

Chapter 2

[1]Now Naomi had a relative on her husband's side, from the clan of Elimelech, a man of standing, whose name was Boaz.

[2]And Ruth the Moabitess said to Naomi, "Let me go to the fields and pick up the left-over grain behind anyone in whose eyes I find favor."

Naomi said to her, "Go ahead, my daughter." [3]So she went out and began to glean in the fields behind the harvesters. As it turned out, she found herself working in a field belonging to Boaz, who was from the clan of Elimelech.

[4]Just then Boaz arrived from Bethlehem and greeted the harvesters, "The LORD be with you!"

"The LORD bless you!" they called back.

[5]Boaz asked the foreman of his harvesters, "Whose young woman is that?"

[6]The foreman replied, "She is the Moabitess who came back from Moab with Naomi. [7]She said, 'Please let me glean and gather among the sheaves behind the harvesters.' She went into the field and has worked steadily from morning till now, except for a short rest in the shelter."

[8]So Boaz said to Ruth, "My daughter, listen to me. Don't go and glean in another field and don't go away from here. Stay here with my servant girls. [9]Watch the field where the men are harvesting, and follow along after the girls. I have told the men not to touch you. And whenever you are thirsty, go and get a drink from the water jars the men have filled."

[10]At this, she bowed down with her face to the ground. She exclaimed, "Why have I found such favor in your eyes that you notice me—a foreigner?"

[11]Boaz replied, "I've been told all about what you have done for your mother-in-law since the death of your husband—how you left your father and mother and your homeland and came to live with a people you did not know before. [12]May the LORD repay you for what you have done. May you be richly rewarded by the LORD, the God of Israel, under whose wings you have come to take refuge."

[13]"May I continue to find favor in your eyes, my lord," she said. "You have given me comfort and have spoken kindly to your servant—though I do not have the standing of one of your servant girls."

[14]At mealtime Boaz said to her, "Come over here. Have some bread and dip it in the wine vinegar."

When she sat down with the harvesters, he offered her some roasted grain. She ate all she wanted and had some left over. [15]As she got up to glean, Boaz gave orders to his men, "Even if she gathers among the sheaves, don't embarrass her. [16]Rather, pull out some stalks for her from the bundles and leave them for her to pick up, and don't rebuke her."

[17]So Ruth gleaned in the field until evening. Then she threshed the barley she had gathered, and it amounted to about an ephah. [18]She carried it back to town, and her mother-in-law saw how much she had gathered. Ruth also brought out and gave her what she had left over after she had eaten enough.

[19]Her mother-in-law asked her, "Where did you glean today? Where did you work? Blessed be the man who took notice of you!"

Then Ruth told her mother-in-law about the one at whose place she had been working. "The name of the man I worked with today is Boaz," she said.

[20]"The LORD bless him!" Naomi said to her daughter-in-law. "He has not stopped showing his kindness to the living and the dead." She added, "That man is our close relative; he is one of our kinsman-redeemers."

[21]Then Ruth the Moabitess said, "He even said to me, 'Stay with my workers until they finish harvesting all my grain.'"

[22]Naomi said to Ruth her daughter-in-law, "It will be good for you, my daughter, to go with his girls, because in someone else's field you might be harmed."

[23]So Ruth stayed close to the servant girls of Boaz to glean until the barley and wheat harvests were finished. And she lived with her mother-in-law.

Chapter 3

[1]One day Naomi her mother-in-law said to her, "My daughter, should I not try to find a home for you, where you will be well provided for? [2]Is not Boaz, with whose servant girls you have been, a kinsman of ours? Tonight he will be winnowing barley on the threshing floor. [3]Wash and perfume yourself, and put on your best clothes. Then go down to the threshing floor, but don't let him know you are there until he has finished eating and drinking. [4]When he lies down, note the place where he is lying. Then go and uncover his feet and lie down. He will tell you what to do."

[5]"I will do whatever you say," Ruth answered. [6]So she went down to the threshing floor and did everything her mother-in-law told her to do.

[7]When Boaz had finished eating and drinking and was in good spirits, he went over to lie down at the far end of the grain pile. Ruth approached quietly, uncovered his feet and lay down. [8]In the middle of the night something startled the man, and he turned and discovered a woman lying at his feet.

[9]"Who are you?" he asked.

"I am your servant Ruth," she said. "Spread the corner of your garment over me, since you are a kinsman-redeemer."

[10]"The LORD bless you, my daughter," he replied. "This kindness is greater than that which you showed earlier: You have not run after the younger men, whether rich or poor. [11]And now, my daughter, don't be afraid. I will do for you all you ask. All my fellow townsmen know that you are a woman of noble character. [12]Although it is true that I am near of kin, there is a kinsman-redeemer nearer than I. [13]Stay here for the night, and in the morning if he wants to redeem, good; let him redeem. But if he is not willing, as surely as the LORD lives I will do it. Lie here until morning."

¹⁴So she lay at his feet until morning, but got up before anyone could be recognized; and he said, "Don't let it be known that a woman came to the threshing floor."

¹⁵He also said, "Bring me the shawl you are wearing and hold it out." When she did so, he poured into it six measures of barley and put it on her. Then he went back to town.

¹⁶When Ruth came to her mother-in-law, Naomi asked, "How did it go, my daughter?" Then she told her everything Boaz had done for her ¹⁷and added, "He gave me these six measures of barley, saying, 'Don't go back to your mother-in-law empty-handed.' "

¹⁸Then Naomi said, "Wait, my daughter, until you find out what happens. For the man will not rest until the matter is settled today."

Chapter 4

¹Meanwhile Boaz went up to the town gate and sat there. When the kinsman-redeemer he had mentioned came along, Boaz said, "Come over here, my friend, and sit down." So he went over and sat down.

²Boaz took ten of the elders of the town and said, "Sit here," and they did so. ³Then he said to the kinsman-redeemer, "Naomi, who has come back from Moab, is selling the piece of land that belonged to our brother Elimelech. ⁴I thought I should bring the matter to your attention and suggest that you buy it in the presence of these seated here and in the presence of the elders of my people. If you will redeem it, do so. But if you will not, tell me, so I will know. For no one has the right to do it except you, and I am next in line."

"I will redeem it," he said.

⁵Then Boaz said, "On the day you buy the land from Naomi and from Ruth the Moabitess, you acquire the dead man's widow, in order to maintain the name of the dead with his property."

⁶At this, the kinsman-redeemer said, "Then I cannot redeem it because I might endanger my own estate. You redeem it yourself. I cannot do it."

⁷(Now in earlier times in Israel, for the redemption and transfer of property to become final, one party took off his sandal and gave it to the other. This was the method of legalizing transactions in Israel.)

⁸So the kinsman-redeemer said to Boaz, "Buy it yourself." And he removed his sandal.

⁹Then Boaz announced to the elders and all the people, "Today you are witnesses that

I have bought from Naomi all the property of Elimelech, Kilion and Mahlon. ¹⁰I have also acquired Ruth the Moabitess, Mahlon's widow, as my wife, in order to maintain the name of the dead with his property, so that his name will not disappear from among his family or from the town records. Today you are witnesses!"

¹¹Then the elders and all those at the gate said, "We are witnesses. May the LORD make the woman who is coming into your home like Rachel and Leah, who together built up the house of Israel. May you have standing in Ephrathah and be famous in Bethlehem. ¹²Through the offspring the LORD gives you by this young woman, may your family be like that of Perez, whom Tamar bore to Judah."

¹³So Boaz took Ruth and she became his wife. Then he went to her, and the LORD enabled her to conceive, and she gave birth to a son. ¹⁴The women said to Naomi: "Praise be to the LORD, who this day has not left you without a kinsman-redeemer. May he become famous throughout Israel! ¹⁵He will renew your life and sustain you in your old age. For your daughter-in-law, who loves you and who is better to you than seven sons, has given him birth."

¹⁶Then Naomi took the child, laid him in her lap and cared for him. ¹⁷The women living there said, "Naomi has a son." And they named him Obed. He was the father of Jesse, the father of David.

¹⁸This, then, is the family line of Perez:

Perez was the father of Hezron,
¹⁹Hezron the father of Ram,
Ram the father of Amminadab,
²⁰Amminadab the father of Nahshon,
Nahshon the father of Salmon,
²¹Salmon the father of Boaz,
Boaz the father of Obed,
²²Obed the father of Jesse,
and Jesse the father of David.